THE MANHOOD PROJECT

CURRICULUM MANUAL

PHIL BLACK
Author, Mentor, and Founder of The Manhood Project

Phil Black is an Author, Inspirational Speaker, and the Founder of The Manhood Project (TMP). The Manhood Project is a coaching and personal development program designed to maximize the positive qualities of young men, while minimizing their temptations to engage in at-risk behavior. The program focuses on character building, development of communication skills, and personal exploration.

Like many young men, Phil was raised in a single-parent home by his mother. Though she did everything a child could hope for in raising him, the absence of his father left more questions than answers as he searched for guidance while becoming a man. Over the years, Phil faced countless emotional and physical challenges. On September 27th in 1997, he nearly lost his life to an act of gun violence. That incident changed Phil's life forever and in many ways, became the driving force behind his work today.

Prior to creating TMP, Phil worked with an internationally recognized, education based nonprofit called City Year, LLC. There, he was able to use his background in Learning & Development to enhance staff and volunteer performance. Phil has also served as a Senior Program Manager, Learning & Development Expert, and National Sales Trainer. Phil's most recent position has been a lead trainer with PEAR (Program in Education and Resilience), helping him accrue more than a decade in of experience in youth training.

In addition to his work with TMP, Phil (or "Coach Black") holds dual certifications as a Life Strategies Coach and Youth Leadership Coach. Phil is a member of the BMe Community, founded by Trabian Shorters (formerly of the Knight Foundation), and is a member of the Detroit City Council's Task Force on Black Male Engagement.

Past awards and recognition include: the Omega Psi Phi Fraternity Inc. Uplift Award for Community Service, Citizen of the Year Award from Clark Preparatory Academy, the 2013 BMe Community Leadership Award, Two time Spirit of Detroit Award recipient, the 2015 Torch of Wisdom Award winner for Scholarship, and his latest accomplishment- the recipient of the Presidential Award for Service.

"Manhood is about being present, not perfect." –Phil Black

THE MANHOOD PROJECT
CURRICULUM GUIDE

Phil Black
2051 Rosa Parks Boulevard
Suite 1B
Detroit, Michigan 48216
www.tmpmentoring.com

Printed in the United States of America

Publisher's Cataloging-in-Publication data
Black, Phil
TMP Curriculum Guide / Phil Black; with major contributions by Celeste Davis
p. cm.
ISBN 978-0-9979817-0-4
1. Education —History —Other category. 2. Another subject Social Science—From one perspective. 3. More categories —
HF0000.A0 A00 2010

"Manhood is about being present, not perfect." –Phil Black

DEDICATION

I dedicate this book to every individual who has the heart and mind to build others. Anyone can share knowledge and information, but only a chosen few will do so with genuine care and from a loving spirit. Not everyone will be you.

"Manhood is about being present, not perfect." –Phil Black

ACKNOWLEDGEMENTS

I owe a great deal of appreciation to several individuals and organizations for their contributions, support, and inspiration in bringing this project to fruition.

To Celeste Davis, thank you for your wonderful input and contributions to this text. You helped bring my vision to life and for that, I am forever grateful.

To my incredible editor Lisa Erby, thank you for not only taking on this project- but for doing so with the love, care, and enthusiasm as if it were your very own project. This would not have been complete without you.

To my fellow brothers of BMe Community- know that your unwavering commitment to our community and uplifting of Black Men in our society inspires me daily.

To my uncles- Billy, Rodney, Jerry and the late Kenneth Black-, words cannot express the appreciation and sheer gratitude I have for the examples that you have been in my life. Each of you, in your own way, made the decision to stand in the gap and help raise someone else's boy into a man. I would not be here, if not for all of you.

Lastly, to my boys, MY young brothers- the young men of The Manhood Project. While I started this program in an effort to give, I am thankful for all that I have received. Seeing you all grow, learn and discover self- has been more rewarding than I could have possibly imagined. Thank you for allowing me into your space and lives, as you continue your journey. I love you all.

"Manhood is about being present, not perfect." –Phil Black

"Manhood is about being present, not perfect." –Phil Black

The Manhood Project Curriculum Guide

Introduction... 5

The Manhood Project At A Glance...................................8

The Five Virtues of Manhood.......................................10

The Creed of Men...13

Curriculum Overview..14
    Session Format... 15
    Unit Overviews..16

    Unit 1 Defining Manhood and Self-Image...................17
    Background and Overview......................................18
    Lesson Plans and Materials...................................19

    Session 1:   Establishing Norms, Expectations, and Goal setting.............20
    Session 2:   Building a Positive and Inclusive Environment...................26
    Session 3:   Defining Manhood..32
    Session 4:   At-Risk Behavior...37
    Session 5:   My Image and I..43
    Session 6:   My Image and I, PT II....................................48
    Session 7:   Unit 1 Review...56
    Session 8:   Assessment, Recognition, and Reflection.......................60

    Unit 2 Communication..66
    Background and Overview......................................67
    Lesson Plans and Materials...................................68

    Session 9:   Guest Speaker(s)...69
    Session 10:   Student One-on-Ones......................................70
    Session 11:   Communication 101- Defining Communication...................71
    Session 12:   Communication 102- Environments and Individuals.............77
    Session 13:   Communication and Technology.............................83
    Session 14:   Understanding Communicative Spaces........................90
    Session 15:   Reputation Impact..95
    Session 16:   Assessment, Recognition, and Reflection......................107

    Unit 3 The Choice: Education or Prison......................111
    Unit 3 Background and Overview..............................112
    Lesson Plans and Materials...................................113

    Session 17:   Guest Speaker(s)...114
    Session 18:   Student One-on-Ones......................................116

"Manhood is about being present, not perfect." –Phil Black

Session 19:   Prison Pipeline 1...118
                     Slavery by Another Name Worksheet...........................122
Session 20:   Buying Habits...125
                     My Favorites Worksheet.....................................131
                     Buying Habits Worksheet....................................132
Session 21:   Post Assessment...135
Session 22:   Prison Pipeline (Pop Culture)................................140
Session 23:   Assessing and Selecting Your Circle.........................145
Session 24:   Assessment, Recognition and Reflection......................154

Unit 4 The Importance of Showing Up (Presence Over Perfection).............158
Background and Overview..159
Lesson Plans and Materials.....................................160

Session 25:   Guest Speaker(s)..161
Session 26:   Student One-on-Ones...162
Session 27:   Be Present..163
Session 28:   Pursuit of Happiness..165
Session 29:   My Support...168
Session 30:   Outreach Activity/Community Engagement.....................176
Session 31:   Service Debrief...178
Session 32:   Assessment, Recognition and Reflection......................183

Unit 5 Living the Five Virtues..185
Background and Overview..186
Lesson Plans and Materials.....................................187

Session 33:   Guest Speaker(s)..188
Session 34:   Student One-on-Ones...189
Session 35:   Establishing a Moral Code....................................191
Session 36:   Love...199
Session 37:   Respect...207
Session 38:   Respect (Part II)..210
Session 39:   Respect (Part III)...214
Session 40:   Courage, Provision, and Protection..........................223
Session 41:   Assessment, Recognition, and Reflection.....................232

Unit 6 Discipline, Self-Guidance, and Leadership...............................235
Background and Overview..236
Lesson Plans and Materials.....................................237

Session 42:   Guest Speaker(s)..238
Session 43:   Student One-on-Ones...240
Session 44:   My Journey...241
Session 45:   Leadership...249
Session 46:   Motivation 101..254
                     "*If*" by Rudyard Kipling.....................................259

"Manhood is about being present, not perfect." –Phil Black

Session 47:   Inspiration...260
Session 48:   Lesson Plan Template (Plan Your Own Session).............264
Session 49:   Lesson Plan Template......................................266

Resources...270
TMP Group Norms..271
Parting Pledge...272
Lesson Plan Template...273
BONUS SESSION: Locker Room...276

Guest Speaker(s)...277
Guest Speaker(s) Template..278
Speaker Question Guide..279
Facilitation/Guest Speaker(s) Tips...281
Guest Speaker Student Notes..282

One-on-Ones..283
Initial One-on-One Template...285
On-going One-on-One Template..286
I AM...289
I am NOT...290
Letter to Self...291
My Values...235
Assessing My Rep...295
Permission Slip Example..297
Notes..298

"Manhood is about being present, not perfect." –Phil Black

"Manhood is about being present, not perfect." –Phil Black

Introduction

The **MISSION** of The Manhood Project (*TMP*) is to maximize the positive qualities of underserved young men, while minimizing temptations to engage in at-risk behavior.

Phil Black, affectionately known as Coach Black, created The Manhood Project as a testimony to the positive role models that he encountered throughout his own youth. Acknowledging the significant impact that mentorship instilled in his life, truly helped fuel Coach Blacks' need to extend that same assistance to young men in communities across the country. Knowing that mentorship was vital to the success of future generations, the birth of TMP became crucial.

Coach Black's personal journey has allowed him to create TMP using his own triumphs and challenges as a guide to assist young boys in leading full and productive lives. Raised by his single mother in Detroit and Highland Park, Michigan, Coach Black has overcome countless personal, professional, and spiritual hurdles. Those once private hurdles, now made public as a result of his testimony- include a failed suicide attempt at the age of nine- a result of major depression, as well as surviving a near-death shooting as a college student. Coach Black's' first book: "From Me to You- A Memoir," is the quintessential testimony, as it truly embodies the need for TMP based curriculum.

Using those life experiences as his platform, Coach Black uses his emotional scars, as well as the help of those that have mentored him in the past, as motivation to help others grow and heal. Over time, Coach Black has achieved and continues to maintain a reputation built on honesty, integrity, and professionalism. His background in youth development magnifies his credibility, as his resume speaks for itself. As an advocate for youth and young adults, Coach Black has multiple certifications, more than ten years of experience in learning and youth development, and has been a lead trainer with PEAR (Program in Education and Resilience). As the recipient of the Presidential Award for Service, Coach Black continues to maintain wonderful relationships between students, families and schools throughout his community. One of his biggest strengths includes communication- which is essential when building relationships between mentors and mentees. His thought provoking, straight-forward, conversational approach when communicating, captures the attention of his mentee and cultivates a relationship built on effective listening and honesty. Through The Manhood Project, Coach Black inspires and challenges communities to be more proactive and aid in improving the lives of those within their communities.

> *"Mentoring, at its core, guarantees young people that there is someone who cares about them, assures them they are not alone in dealing with day-to-day challenges, and makes them feel like they matter. Research confirms that quality mentoring relationships have powerful positive effects on young people in a variety of personal, academic, and professional situations. Ultimately, mentoring connects a young person to personal growth and development, and social and economic opportunity. Yet one in three young people will grow up without this critical asset."*

-Mentor.org

"Manhood is about being present, not perfect." –Phil Black

That's where you come in. Yes, **YOU**.

We know you. You've recognized a **need** relating to your communities population of underserved young men. You want to make a **change**. You know that it will take some **structure, discipline and guidance**- *you're just asking how to get started*.

Well, this curriculum has been designed specifically for you.

This curriculum serves as a guide to **educators** and **community volunteers** alike, to assist in the implementation of the core lessons of TMP into afterschool and extracurricular activities. This curriculum provides a **shell** for you to build and customize *your own unique TMP-based program,* according to the needs of the young men that require your mentorship. We've created the framework that allows you, as the facilitator, the flexibility to integrate your own ideas and methodology into weekly lessons. In each unit and lesson plan (customizable), you'll receive structured suggestions, however, you have 100% autonomy over your presentation and programming, as long as the core values are maintained and align with the vision and structure of The Manhood Project.

From this point on, all we require from you is continued commitment, passion, patience, an open-mind, leadership, fun, and of course- love.

Manhood is about being present- not perfect.

Let's get started.

"Manhood is about being present, not perfect." –Phil Black

**"You are the bows from which your children as living arrows are sent forth.
The archer sees the mark upon the path of the infinite, and He bends you with His might
that His arrows may go swift and far.
Let your bending in the archer's hand be for gladness;
For even as He loves the arrow that flies, so He loves also the bow that is stable."**

-Kahlil Gibran, The Prophet

"Manhood is about being present, not perfect." –Phil Black

The Manhood Project at a Glance

TMP's Background

The Manhood Project is a **COACHING AND PERSONAL DEVELOPMENT PROGRAM** specifically designed for young men.

The Manhood Project, based on the belief that underserved young men have **just as much potential** to succeed as anyone else, was conceived in 2011, by Coach Black. TMP breeds successful young men by a proven formula that includes: exposing them to **positive environments**, aligning them with empathetic **mentors**, equipping them with the right **tools** for success, and showing those same young men **possible future outcomes** if fully committed to themselves and direction from The Manhood Project. Through perseverance and positive interpersonal relationships, the end result will always be **extraordinary change**. In order for our young men to experience change and have positive outcomes in life, programs like TMP must exist to educate and promote their success, rather than enable their demise.

Without programs like TMP, those young men deemed "at-risk" will continue to be neglected, ostracized and headed for negative future outcomes. This is why mentorship and community oriented service programs are needed. The majority of those young men in need of TMP's curriculum, began life behind their more affluent counterparts. Being raised in single parent households, residing in low-income areas riddled with crime, attending under resourced schools within districts that are continuing to combat high dropout rates- are just a short list of examples of **why** TMP's curriculum is needed. This curriculum can level the playing field for young men in need of assistance, and completely transform their lives. This guide is not exclusive to young men that are disadvantaged. Our curriculum is designed to meet the needs of students coming from two parent households that *appear* to have an abundance of resources, but fall short on the guidance and mentorship provided by TMP. These future leaders need examples, mentorship, and accountability partners to show them exactly what their future can be with the right attitude, support system and the most important element: belief in self.

In recent years, mentoring programs that target young people of disadvantaged backgrounds have become more prevalent in community outreach initiatives. With the creation of programs like President Obama's: My Brother's Keeper, there is a large push to eliminate the opportunity gap between men of color and non-Hispanic white men. The elimination of opportunity gaps can lead to a higher quality of life, lower rates of incarceration, and healthier, better educated adults. More information about why these programs are important can be found on The White House's summary of Economic Costs of Youth Disadvantage and High-Return Opportunities for Change.

"Manhood is about being present, not perfect." –Phil Black

How exactly does The Manhood Project assist these young men in succeeding at life?

*Using a modular curriculum structure, TMP introduces and reinforces concepts of leadership development, while aiding in the personal growth of its participants, by implementing a **four-part approach** to coaching and personal development.*

EXPOSURE:	EDUCATION:
Change requires exposure to unfamiliar environments, lifestyles and ways of thinking. To begin the process of change in our young men, TMP connects each student with real individuals (outside of TMP leadership) to aide in their personal development and growth. Students will also engage with positive and impactful speakers that share their personal stories of struggle and triumph. Additionally, TMP matches students with social excursions that will supplement and enhance classroom curriculum.	TMP provides structured, educational workshops- based off of the core areas of development and learning. Dr. Gill Noam, professor at Harvard University and founder of the PEAR Institute (Partnerships in Education And Resilience), has identified four essential "ingredients" required for growth in all learners. Those four ingredients, derived from extensive developmental research, are: **active engagement, assertiveness, belonging, and reflection**. TMP lesson plans provide opportunities for learners to: be physically engaged, share and develop their own voice, work collaboratively while giving space for students to make meaning through guided reflection.
ENGAGEMENT:	ENCOURAGEMENT:
TMP engages students in service-learning, civic engagement opportunities, as well as activities that build character and overall growth (e.g. peer mentoring with younger students, community beautification projects).	TMP will acknowledge, observe, and course-correct each students progress. Positive affirmations will be reinforced as students continue to make greater and sustainable gains.

"Manhood is about being present, not perfect." –Phil Black

Using the four part modular curriculum approach, all TMP activities focus on:

Self-Discovery: *Becoming aware of one's true potential, character, motives, etc.*

We do this because students cannot course correct or make well-informed decisions until they understand their own nature, feelings, reactions, and past experiences. Once the student embarks on their personal self-discovery journey, they are more than likely to **not** return to their former ways.

Influencing behavior: By addressing the root cause, problematic behavior can be corrected. Building off of self-discovery, we specifically focus on influencing behavior by providing alternative responses. Once a student has been exposed to various points of view, they are then empowered to see events from a logical (rather than emotional) perspective. This change of response equips the student to selectively choose their future responses to difficult situations, rather than react emotionally to them. Once the student has been assessed, a plan is put into motion to prevent barriers, address and acknowledge root causes, so that the student succeeds and continues positive relationship-building.

Social skills: Development of skillsets that facilitate interaction and communication with others. Social rules are created, communicated, and changed in verbal and nonverbal ways. We accomplish this through guided discussions, role play and other activities.

While it appears that we focus heavily on inward development, we are well aware that outward development grows in tandem- both adversely affecting social skills. Social skills are important as they allow students to positively advocate on their behalf and aid in maintaining a healthy social life.

School and community engagement: Participation and involvement in activities within regular social environments. Community service teaches compassion, understanding, encourages social interactions, builds problem solving skills, aids in academia and gives students the opportunity to network.

Service is a principle that we believe is essential for ensuring self-growth and awareness. Students involved in service benefit from the experience and invest in their communities. Our participants will learn to balance engagement activities with other activities as a regular part of their daily lives. This balance is beneficial to their lifetime survival skills.

"Manhood is about being present, not perfect." –Phil Black

What will participants take away from the program?
By the end of the program the participants will be able to:

- ❑ Recite and understand the <u>Five Virtues</u> (Love, Respect, Courage, Provision, and Protection).

- ❑ Recite the <u>Creed of Man</u>, while expressing its value.

- ❑ Identify, develop and maintain a healthy self-concept. This is achieved when one has a positive image of self, and is leading a life that is consistently aligned with their personal values.

- ❑ Recognize appropriate and inappropriate behaviors and individuals, within their environment.

- ❑ Practice reflective and gained communication skills, to minimize at-risk behaviors while increasing the likelihood of academic success, and leading productive lives.

The Manhood Project uses different learning styles to present and reinforce the lessons in the curriculum.

Elements of a MultiSensory Lesson
TMP lessons are themed, written and delivered to connect to the learner's senses and emotions. Each unit of study is planned and detailed to allow the learner to connect to the material in a more visceral fashion.

Setting Up the Classroom Environment for All Learning Styles
Environmental stimuli has a significant impact on the learner. TMP lessons encourage a classroom set up that encourages group engagement during all activities. Desk arrangements that facilitate open communication and direct eye contact are extremely important. Distracting stimuli and objects within the classroom are put away to avoid disruption during learning.

"Manhood is about being present, not perfect." –Phil Black

The Five Virtues of Manhood

Love
Learning to love yourself makes it possible to love others.

Respect
When you give respect, you are more likely to receive it.

Courage
Courage is about having the strength to be yourself, no matter what you face or who is watching.

Provision
Every man must possess the ability and willingness to provide for himself and for his family.

Protection
We must protect all that has been entrusted to us. Especially those who cannot protect themselves.

"Manhood is about being present, not perfect." –Phil Black

Creed of Men

We love according to the commandment.
We know respect must start from within, given and earned, before it can be received.
We are courageous enough to be ourselves and not follow the negative influences of others.
We vow to provide for our households while helping others in need.
We protect all that is entrusted to our care and those who cannot defend themselves.
In times of fear and doubt, we remind ourselves and each other:
"You don't have to be perfect, but you must be present."

For these are the measures of a man

"Manhood is about being present, not perfect." –Phil Black

Curriculum Overview

Our **curriculum** guides participants through lessons that will initiate a deeper understanding of self and ultimately lead to happy and productive lives. Here, you'll find templates for **customizable** lessons and activities. These are to be used as a guide for you and are completely **flexible**. The only requirement is that the **intent** of the lesson stays– as our methodology and approach is based off of research and on-going assessments of TMP graduates.

Each unit allows time for one on one coaching sessions with students, guest speakers, and field trips. Templates are included for these as well.

Included in each lesson plan are slots for the facilitator to strategize unique lessons of their own. You'll see the space within the lessons for you to take the lead in providing assessments, reviews, introductions, and other educational content.

Before beginning a lesson, you'll need to review the lesson plan, making sure that all materials are available, and that talking points are ready. These talking points are outlined for each lesson, and can be tweaked to your liking. Each session also follows a similar format that is essential for a full, well-rounded, and interactive lesson.

"Manhood is about being present, not perfect." –Phil Black

Session Format

A template for session lesson plans will be included in the resource section of this guide. In this section, you'll find descriptions of important **elements** that provide both structure and consistency for the learner during each session. Each element should be included in order to create a safe and positive space for students to learn, absorb and apply the information presented.

Snack and Chat: It is important to allow students to engage freely with one another throughout the day. Snack and chat has been designated for students to simply unwind from the day, share stories regarding lessons learned, and simply engage in general conversation. While Snack and Chat appears futile, this time is crucial for an uninterrupted learning environment. Should a student attend a session while hungry, that student is less likely to concentrate and focus. Students suffering from chronic hunger can experience memory issues as well as psychological effects that can deter them from proper learning. Students attending sessions depending upon the total time of the session, we designate 6 to 12 minutes for Snack & Chat or roughly 5 to 8 percent of the session time.

Note: this time should be uninterrupted by the facilitator. This time is imperative to refuel energy, meet basic needs, and captivate attention for the lesson.

Highlights or Do-Overs (H & D's): H & D's are a quick way for the facilitator to engage students about life outside of the program. Participants verbally volunteer one highlight and/or a "do-over" they've experienced since their last session. A *highlight* could be something as simple as a meal at their favorite restaurant, family get together, or outing with friends. A *do-over* is an event or situation that occurred within the student's life that in retrospect, he recognizes he could've handled differently. The goal in reliving do-overs is to challenge the student to correct past behaviors, and continue acting positively to yield a better outcome (examples include: an argument, low grade on a test, etc.).

Review: A brief review of the material from the previous session to ensure students are ready to move forward learning new material.

Warm-up: An activity or discussion that helps to prepare students for the lesson of the day.

Lesson: New material.

Recap: Review of the new material.

Reflection: A probing question to help merge newly learned material into their everyday perspective and outlook.

Close: Each lesson should end with the closing pledge (and all activities) before parting ways. The pledge should be memorized by the participants and facilitator as soon as possible. The pledge should be recited while the group locks arms and makes a circle.

"Manhood is about being present, not perfect." –Phil Black

Unit Overviews

Unit I: Defining Manhood and Self Image
Lesson plans will:
- ❑ Establish norms, expectations, and goal setting for program participation
- ❑ Help participants define a positive, healthy meaning for manhood
- ❑ Guide students through a reflection of behavior and self-image

Unit II: Appropriate Communication
Lesson plans will:
- ❑ Differentiate between the types of communication
- ❑ Help participants build tools for healthy communication
- ❑ Practice healthy communication methods

Unit III: Prison Pipeline
Lesson plans will:
- ❑ Give background on School to Prison Pipeline
- ❑ Help participants understand current systems landscape
- ❑ Give students tools to advocate for themselves and their peers

Unit IV: The Importance of Showing Up (Presence Over Perfection)
Lesson plans will:
- ❑ Help participants establish behaviors of responsibility and commitment
- ❑ Cultivate acts of service to others in the community
- ❑ Exercise consistency and reliability in activities

Unit V: Living the Five Virtues
Lesson plans will:
- ❑ Explore TMP's Five Virtues of Manhood
- ❑ Understand the importance of the Five Virtues
- ❑ Learn how to implement the Five Virtues in daily life practice

Unit VI: Discipline, Self-Guidance, and Leadership
Lesson plans will:
- ❑ Give students tools to execute positive behavior change
- ❑ Provide methods for students to support and encourage others to exhibit positive behaviors
- ❑ Create long-lasting positive and impactful behavior

"Manhood is about being present, not perfect." –Phil Black

Unit 1: Defining Manhood and Self Image

"Try not to become a man of success, but rather try to become a man of value."

-Albert Einstein

"Manhood is about being present, not perfect." –Phil Black

Unit 1 Background and Overview

This unit sets the foundation for the facilitator and participants, as they establish intentions for one another. As a facilitator, you are introducing the participants to the program and introducing them to the *concept* of **manhood**. *Note to facilitator: It is not their role or the intent of this information to give the learner a prescribed definition of manhood, rather we are working to guide them in the process of defining it for themselves- according to their personal values and desired life goals.* As participants, the boys are reflecting on their own self-image, how it may relate to manhood- while introducing themselves to you and their peers within the room.

This concept is called **level setting**. The purpose of level setting is to get everyone on the same page, set the tone for expectations- not only in this unit, but in the weeks to come.

First, we set the tone by setting expectations of how we'll interact with one another and what results we want from this program. Next, we'll start to look inward and delve into self-reflection and building self-awareness.

SESSIONS included within this unit:

SESSION 1:   Establishing Norms, Expectations, and Goal Setting
SESSION 2:   Building a Positive and Inclusive Environment
SESSION 3:   Defining Manhood
SESSION 4:   At Risk Behavior
SESSION 5:   My Image and I
SESSION 6:   My Image and I (pt. II)
SESSION 7:   Unit 1 Review
SESSION 8:   Assessment, Recognition, and Reflection

"Manhood is about being present, not perfect." –Phil Black

Lesson Plans + Materials

"Manhood is about being present, not perfect." –Phil Black

SESSION 1: Establishing Norms, Expectations, and Goal Setting

Unit   S1: Session Objectives

By the end of this session the learner will be able to:

1. Determine acceptable and unacceptable conduct within the TMP space.

2. Recognize and identify the operational and communicative group norms.

3. Identify expectations. What is expected of them (e.g. conduct, behavior changes) as a result of participating in the program.

4. Communicate short (e.g. end of Unit I) and long-term (e.g. end of the program) goals for themselves.

AGENDA

1. Sign-in

2. Snack & Chat

3. Welcome

4. Warm-up

5. Pre Assessment

6. Introduction
   - Who are we?
   - What is The Manhood Project (TMP)?

7. Session Introduction
   - Overview
   - Objectives
   - Agenda

8. Lesson
   - Activity
   - Recap
   - Norms
   - Expectations

9. Close
   - Post-Assessment

"Manhood is about being present, not perfect." –Phil Black

- Clean-up
- Reflection
- Announcements
- Parting Pledge

ACTIVITIES

1. Warm-Up: Birthday Circle
2. Worst of Times/Best of Times

ROOM SET-UP	MATERIALS NEEDED
Full or Half Circle Seating	1. Flipchart Paper 2. Dry Erase Board 3. Printing Paper 4. Markers 5. Pens 6. Small or Medium Size Ball (for tossing)

SESSION PREP

1. Ensure that the sign-in sheet is ready.

2. Print:
   - Pre and post assessments
   - Copies of opening and closing pledge

3. Set-up transition music.

4. Make sure snacks are ready for distribution.

5. *Write* and post: Objectives, Agenda, Norms & Expectations, and Review Questions on separate sheets of flipchart paper. *If Dry Erase Board is available, use it to write session objectives. Reserve flipchart for other information.*

6. Pre-determine the number of groups you would like to have for the Worst/Best activity (Ex: 4 groups of 3). Select one sheet of flipchart paper per group. Draw a line down the middle of the page, dividing it into two sections. Write "Worst" on the left, and "Best" on the right of the line (at the top of the sheet). Post the flipcharts on the wall in different areas of the room maintaining space between each group.

"Manhood is about being present, not perfect." –Phil Black

		SESSION DETAILS
1.5 - 2 hr		
	Pre-Session	Set up all materials and music
3 mins	**Sign-in**	Have students sign in as they enter the space
8 mins	**Snack & Chat**	Note: Once participants have become accustomed to the session format and routine, Snack & Chat may shift based on your observation or the group's needs. Example: During session 8, you sense a need to get students moving due to low energy. Instead of beginning with Snack & Chat, you go right into the warm-up and reserve Snack & Chat for after.
3 mins	**Welcome**	Thank students for coming and introduce the warm-up
12 mins	**Warm up: Birthday Circle**	Begin with the warm up exercise titled, Birthday Circle. 1. Direct students to form a circle. 2. Once the circle has been formed, have students rearrange themselves according to their birthday month. *Note: Do not give any additional clarity, the purpose is for students to mingle with one another to find out each other's birthday month.* 3. Finally, using the ball (as the talking ball) have students introduce themselves by: Name, Birthday Month, and grade. Once a student has shared, they may toss the ball to anyone in the circle. Repeat until each participant has completed an introduction.
(optional)	**Highlights and Do-Overs**	At any time, feel free to introduce your own conversation starter (ice breaker) or activity to build rapport/team.
3 mins	**Session Introduction**	1. Overview: Our first session is simply about getting to know one another, gaining an understanding of the program, and what is expected. 2. Objectives: Have a volunteer read the objectives. Provide any clarity you feel is needed. 3. Agenda: After the objectives have been covered, reveal and recite the agenda.
35 mins	**Lesson**	<u>What is TMP?</u>

"Manhood is about being present, not perfect." –Phil Black

Begin by explaining the fundamental information of TMP (*or your program*).

1. What is The Manhood Project (TMP)? TMP is a coaching/mentoring program specifically designed for young men.

2. The motto of the program is "To be a man you don't have to be perfect, but you do have to be present."

3. Program virtues:
   This is a great space to engage, by asking students to define what a virtue is?
   -The TMP virtues are (in order): Love, Respect, Courage, Provision, and Protection.

Transition:
Please commit this information to memory, as it is an integral part of the program. Further information will be provided as we move throughout the curriculum.

Activity: Worst of Times/Best of Times
The objective of this activity is to have students reflect/act out their worst/best classroom experience, relating to student conduct. The goal is to have them self-identify both unacceptable and acceptable behaviors while working within a classroom.

Steps:
1. Have students count off by the (predetermined) number of groups set for the Worst/Best Activity. (1 min)

2. Instruct students to think about the worst class they've participated in. Have students share their experience within their group. (6 mins)
   Guided Questions:
   What happened (e.g. fight, disruptive behavior)?
   Why did it bother you?
   Did it affect you for the duration of the class?

3. After everyone has shared their stories, have each person write their main issue on the flipchart under "Worst." (Ex: Students were loud and would not stop talking) (3 mins)

4. Have students share what they listed. (5 mins)

5. Repeat Steps 2 and 3 for the "Best" side (or their best experience). (6 mins)

"Manhood is about being present, not perfect." –Phil Black

		Guided Questions What did you enjoy about your best experience? Describe student's behavior. 6. Repeat Step 4 for their best experience. Follow-Up (3 mins) Ask: Who can tell us the purpose of that exercise? *Desired answer: To separate acceptable versus unacceptable behavior.* Main Point: Now that we have established what is unacceptable, we are going to commit to modeling only those behaviors that are acceptable.
6 mins	**Break**	*Set up quiz questions
3 mins	**Recap/Quiz**	Ask each question one by one. After a student shares the answer, ask if everyone agrees or disagrees. *Suggested Questions: (1) "Manhood is about being _____, and not being _____. (2) The Five Virtues are: Love, _____, Courage, Provision, and _____. (3) Describe the type of behavior you are expected to model.
8 mins	**Norms & Expectations**	1. Introduce the group norms and their meanings. 2. Share the expectations you have outlined for your group.
25 mins	**Close**	Post-Assessment: Have students complete the post assessment. (6 mins) Clean-up (4 mins) Reflection: Have each learner share one thing that they've learned. (10 mins) Announcements (2 mins) Parting Pledge (2 mins)

"Manhood is about being present, not perfect." –Phil Black

Session 1 Post Assessment

1. List two people's names and birthday months:

    Name _____ Birthday _____

    Name _____ Birthday _____

2. What does NOSTUESO stand for?

3. Man Law means:

4. The Manhood Project is a _____ and _____ development program.

5. The motto of The Manhood Project is, "You don't have to be _____, but you do have to be _____."

6. The Five Virtues of Manhood are:
    1. _____
    2. _____
    3. _____
    4. _____
    5. _____

7. Give two examples of poor class behavior.

8. Describe what acceptable class behavior is.

"Manhood is about being present, not perfect." –Phil Black

SESSION 2: Building a Positive and Inclusive Environment

Unit 1   S2: Session Objectives

By the end of this session the learner will be able to:

1. Appropriately introduce themselves to various individuals.

2. Share facts about at least one person in the group.

3. Express how learning about others affects their own sense of belonging.

4. Demonstrate and explain the TMP norms and communication tools.

AGENDA

1. Sign-in

2. Snack & Chat

3. Review

4. Pre Assessment

5. Warm-up

6. Session Introduction
   - ❏ Overview
   - ❏ Objectives
   - ❏ Agenda

7. Lesson
   - ❏ Activity
   - ❏ Share

8. Close
   - ❏ Post-Assessment
   - ❏ Clean-up
   - ❏ Reflection
   - ❏ Announcements
   - ❏ Parting Pledge

"Manhood is about being present, not perfect." –Phil Black

ACTIVITIES

1. Warm-Up: My Name is…
2. Linking the Chain

ROOM SET-UP	MATERIALS NEEDED
Full or Half Circle Seating	1. Flipchart Paper 2. Dry Erase Board 3. Art Supplies 4. Markers 5. Pens 6. A list of names of each student

SESSION PREP

1. Ensure sign-in sheet is ready.

2. Print:
   - ❏ Pre and Post assessments
   - ❏ Copies of opening and closing pledge
   - ❏ Copies of the roster for each students to use during the activity.

3. Set-up transition music.

4. Make sure snacks are ready for distribution.

5. Write and post: Objectives, Agenda, and Review Questions on separate sheets of flipchart paper. *If Dry Erase Board is available, use it to write session objectives. Reserve flipchart for the other information.*

6. Be prepared to give an example of a proper introduction. (Ex: Hi my name is _____. You are _____? It is great to meet you (repeat name).

7. Illustrate a life map for the "Linking the Chain" Activity.

"Manhood is about being present, not perfect." –Phil Black

SESSION DETAILS		
1.5 - 2 hr		
	Pre-Session	Set up all materials and music.
3 mins	**Sign-in**	Have students sign in as they enter the designated space.
8 mins	**Snack & Chat**	
3 mins	**Welcome**	Thank students for coming and introduce the warm-up
(optional)	**Highlights and Do-Overs**	
6 mins	**Pre Assessment**	The following questions may be answered verbally or written. ❑ What is the proper way to introduce yourself to someone? ❑ Who can share 2-4 things that they have in common with three or more people in this room?

8 - 12 mins	**Warm-up: My Name is…**	1. *Explain*: One simple, yet important aspect of meeting someone is the introduction. How you introduce yourself tells people a lot about who you are.
		
		*Give the following examples:
		  a. *(Holding your head down and mumbling)* Say: If I introduce myself like this ("Hi my name is _____.") What would you think about me as a person?
		
		  b. *(Standing straight up, making eye contact and smiling)* Say: If I introduce myself like this ("Hi my name is _____.") What might you think about me as a person?
		
		  Target answers: timid versus confident
		
		2. *Explain*: When you introduce yourself, you should exude confidence. You do that by:
		  a. Making and maintaining eye contact.
		  b. Giving a firm handshake.
		  c. Smiling and displaying a pleasant demeanor.
		  d. Speaking at an appropriate level (volume).

"Manhood is about being present, not perfect." –Phil Black

		3. Give an example of what a proper introduction should look like. (1) Hi my name is _____. 2) And your name is? 3) It is nice to meet you _____.) 4. Instruct students to introduce themselves to everyone within the room.
6 mins	**Session Introduction**	1. Overview: Today we will take some time to familiarize ourselves with one another. 2. Objectives: Have a volunteer read the objectives. Provide any clarity you feel that is needed. 3. Agenda: After discussing the objectives, the agenda should be revealed and recited.
35 mins	**Lesson**	Activity: Linking the Chain This activity is designed to give students an opportunity to: (1) Express themselves artistically, (2) Share their backgrounds and (3) Identify how each student may be connected with one another. Steps: 1. *Explain*: We are going to do an activity called "Linking the Chain." I will explain the significance of the title once we've completed the activity. 2. Instruct students to draw a "life map." A life map is a timeline using pictures. Using whatever symbols you can think of, draw a picture of who you are. Where and when were you born? Where you currently live. How many siblings you have? What do you like to do for fun? Name a talent you have. What is your best memory growing up? 3. After students finish drawing, have them share their map one by one. *Note: Before sharing instruct the students to do the following: Using their personal copy of the roster, while each student presents their map, remaining students should write down anything that they have in common with the presenter.*
6 mins	**Break**	*Note: While breaks have a fixed position throughout the TMP curriculum, you will need to assess your students regularly to determine where and how often breaks should occur.* *One rule of thumb would be: 5-7 minutes for every 45 minutes of content.*

"Manhood is about being present, not perfect." –Phil Black

8 mins	**Follow-Up**	4. After students return from break, have them share commonalities.
		5. *Explain*: This exercise is called "Linking the Chain" because it helps us identify our commonalities. *(Pointing to the picture of the TMP logo)* Indicate that this is what is behind the logo of the Manhood Project. The chain link represents the fact that we are all connected. *Ask if there are any questions or comments.*
5 mins	**Recap/Quiz**	*Suggested Questions:* 1. Who can demonstrate how men should introduce themselves? 2. Go around the circle and have each person state a fact about one other person. 3. How has sharing your story and learning about others affected you? 4. Recap the Norms (asking them to explain the concept behind each norm).
15 mins	**Close**	Post-Assessment: Have students complete the post assessment. (6 mins) Clean-up (3 mins) Reflection: One word debrief (2 mins) Announcements (2 mins) Parting Pledge (2 mins)

"Manhood is about being present, not perfect." –Phil Black

Session 2 Post Assessment

1. The Manhood Project is a _____ and _____ development program.

2. The Motto of The Manhood Project is: "You don't have to be _____ but you do have to be _____."

3. The Five Virtues of Manhood are:
   1. _____
   2. _____
   3. Courage
   4. Provision
   5. _____

4. List 4 TMP Norms:

   _____   _____

   _____   _____

5. Describe the type of man you want to be seen as.

6. How did the character Chris Gardner, in the movie *Pursuit of Happiness*, demonstrate the motto of The Manhood Project.

"Manhood is about being present, not perfect." –Phil Black

SESSION 3: Defining Manhood

Unit 1 S3: Session Objectives

At the end of this session the learner will be able to:

1. Identify a negative and a positive example of manhood.

2. List the qualities that create a negative image of manhood.

3. Define a poor example of manhood.

4. Express ways to avoid becoming the negative example.

AGENDA

1. Sign-in

2. Snack & Chat

3. Welcome

4. Review

5. Pre Assessment

6. Warm-up

7. Session Introduction
   - ❑ Overview
   - ❑ Objectives
   - ❑ Agenda

8. Lesson
   - ❑ Activity
   - ❑ Share

9. Close
   - ❑ Post-Assessment
   - ❑ Clean-up
   - ❑ Reflection
   - ❑ Announcements
   - ❑ Parting Pledge

"Manhood is about being present, not perfect." –Phil Black

ACTIVITIES

1. Review Activity: Do you know your neighbors?
2. Warm-Up: "The Man"?
3. The Negative

ROOM SET-UP	MATERIALS NEEDED
Full or Half Circle Seating	1. Training/Talking ball 2. Flipchart Paper 3. Dry Erase Board 4. Markers 5. Pens 6. Index Cards

SESSION PREP

1. Ensure sign-in sheet is ready.

2. Print Pre and Post assessments.

3. Set-up transition music.

4. Make sure snacks are ready for distribution.

5. Write and post: Objectives, Agenda, and Review Questions on separate sheets of flipchart paper.
   If Dry Erase Board is available, use it to write session objectives. Reserve flipchart for the other information.

6. Take 8 separate sheets of flipchart paper. At the top of each, write one of the following categories (for the "Negative" activity):
   - ❏ Women
   - ❏ Kids
   - ❏ Teachers
   - ❏ Parents
   - ❏ Elders (older people)
   - ❏ Nerds
   - ❏ Security guards
   - ❏ Bus drivers

"Manhood is about being present, not perfect." –Phil Black

SESSION DETAILS		
1.5 - 2 hr		
	Pre-Session	Set up all materials and music.
3 mins	**Sign-in**	Have students sign in as they enter the designated space.
8 mins	**Snack & Chat**	
3 mins	**Welcome**	Thank students for coming and introduce the warm-up
8 - 15 mins	**Warm up: The Man**	1. Pass out an index card to each student. 2. *Say*: Think of the absolute best example of a man that you can think of. Whether it is a person in your life currently, someone you have previously met- but are no longer in contact with or select a celebrity. 3. Write everything about that person that stands out in your mind, making them the best example of a man. After each person is finished, have the group share their answers.
(optional)	**Highlights and Do-Overs**	
6 - 8 mins	**Review**	Review TMP's fundamental information and group norms.
8 mins	**Lesson**	<u>Activity: The Negative</u> This activity is designed help students separate the negative qualities of manhood from the positive ones. *Say*: In our warm-up we've shared examples of positive qualities of manhood that we have witnessed or experienced first hand. In this exercise, we are going to take a look at the other side of manhood. *Remind students to not use names during the written exercises.* Steps 1. *Explain*: Around the room are 8 different sheets of paper. With your partner from the warm-up, proceed to one of the sheets. Now, think of the worst example(s) of a boy or man that you have encountered. 2. Written on the paper, you will find a type of person.

"Manhood is about being present, not perfect." –Phil Black

		3. Write examples of how you think that type of person (negative qualities) would behave towards the person on the paper. Write whatever comes to mind. 4. When you are finished, move about the room and write something on each paper. After completing the first sheet, you no longer have to remain with your partner.
8 mins	**Break**	While students are on break, gather the sheets, and repost them side-by-side in the front of the room.
18 mins	**Follow-Up**	6. After the students have returned, have them share their thoughts. *Probing questions*: -What comes to mind when you see these behaviors on the board? -How do you think the people feel when they receive the type of treatment listed? *Ask if there are any questions or comments.*
18 mins	**Close**	Post-Assessment: Have students complete the post assessment. (6 mins) Clean-up (3 mins) Reflection: How did today's session change the way you think about your personal behavior? (5 mins) Announcements (2 mins) Parting Pledge (2 mins)

"Manhood is about being present, not perfect." –Phil Black

Session 3 Post Assessment

1. The Five Virtues of Manhood are:
   1. _____
   2. _____
   3. _____
   4. Provision
   5. _____

2. List the TMP Norms
   1. _____   7. _____
   2. _____   8. _____
   3. _____   9. _____
   4. _____   10. _____
   5. _____   11. _____
   6. _____

3. Describe the how your best example of manhood treats others.

4. Describe the differences between you best and worst examples of Manhood.

"Manhood is about being present, not perfect." –Phil Black

SESSION 4: At Risk Behavior

Unit 1   S4: Session Objectives

By the completion of this session the learner will be able to:

1. Express what it means to be at-risk.

2. List examples of at-risk behaviors (ARB's).

3. Communicate what ARB's they've engaged in prior to joining the program.

4. Explain possible short and long- term consequences exemplifying ARB's.

AGENDA

1. Sign-in

2. Snack & Chat

3. Welcome

4. Review

5. Pre Assessment

6. Warm-up

7. Session Introduction
   - ❏ Overview
   - ❏ Objectives
   - ❏ Agenda

8. Lesson
   - ❏ Video
   - ❏ Define terms
   - ❏ Discussion

9. Close
   - ❏ Post-Assessment
   - ❏ Clean-up
   - ❏ Reflection
   - ❏ Announcements
   - ❏ Parting Pledge

"Manhood is about being present, not perfect." –Phil Black

ACTIVITIES

1. Review Activity:
2. Warm-Up: Biggest Fan
3. Video: Beyond Scared Straight

ROOM SET-UP	MATERIALS NEEDED
Full or Half Circle Seating	1. Video: *Beyond Scared Straight* https://youtu.be/iqMSu_a7gjU 2. Manuals 3. Flipchart Paper 4. Dry Erase Board 5. Markers 6. Pens

SESSION PREP

1. Ensure that the sign-in sheet is ready.

2. Print Pre and Post assessments.

3. Set-up transition music.

4. Make sure snacks are ready for distribution.

5. Set-up audio, visual equipment, and cue video.

6. *Write and post:* Objectives, Agenda, and Review Questions on separate sheets of flipchart paper. *If Dry Erase Board is available, use it to write session objectives. Reserve flipchart for the other information.*

SESSION DETAILS		
1.5 - 2 hr		
	Pre-Session	Set up all materials and music.
3 mins	**Sign-in**	Have students sign in as they enter the designated space.
8 mins	**Snack & Chat**	
3 mins	**Welcome**	Thank students for coming and introduce the warm-up
6 - 8 Mins	**Warm-up: Biggest Fan**	1. Have students select a partner. 2. Each pair will play a game of Rock/Paper/Scissors. Students should play 3 games total, with the winner defeating their opponent in 2 out of the 3 games. 3. The winner moves on to find and play the winner of another pair. 4. The loser then becomes the winner's "Biggest Fan" and has to follow them around cheering their names in the next match. 5. Continue playing as the groups become bigger leaving two players in the end to battle. 6. In the end, the entire group congratulates the last man standing.
(optional)	**Highlights and Do-Overs**	
44 mins	**Lesson**	Video: _Beyond Scared Straight_ 1. _Explain_: The video we are going to watch is called: _Beyond Scared Straight_. This video documents a turnaround program designed to keep young men and women out of prison. _Play video_: _Beyond Scared Straight_
8 mins	**Break**	
		3. Questions: Which story stood out to you and why? Why did Brandon's mother say his actions were a result of being hurt? Which character can you relate to the most? Explain.

"Manhood is about being present, not perfect." –Phil Black

18 mins	**Follow-Up**	*Explain*:
		
		The term "at risk" means exactly what it sounds like. A person is considered at risk of doing or becoming many things based on certain factors or behaviors.
		
		Examples:
		
		   ❑ People can be considered "at risk" of developing a lung disease if they do what?
		      Target answer is smoke
		
		   ❑ You can be considered "at risk" of going to jail if you do what?
		      Target answers include selling drugs
		
		Part of our mission and goal, is to give you an alternative to the behaviors that will put you at risk. Our specific goal is to prevent you from risk factors leading you to drop out of school, which can lead to being poor, and you eventually going to jail.
		
		*Have participants list the following current behaviors that would put them at risk:
		
		1. Fighting
		2. Cursing
		3. Being disruptive in class
		4. Being disrespectful
		5. Joining a gang
		6. Bullying
		7. Skipping class
		8. Getting suspended
		9. Using drugs
		10. Having sex
		
		Ask:
		By a show of hands, how many of you have actually engaged in any of these at risk behaviors?
		
		How do you feel seeing these behaviors listed as at risk? How does this affect you?

4 mins	**Break**	
18 mins	**Close**	Post-Assessment: Have students complete the post assessment. (6 mins) Clean-up (3 mins)

"Manhood is about being present, not perfect." –Phil Black

Reflection: What are some of the short or long term consequences to at risk behavior? (5 mins)

Announcements (2 mins)

Parting Pledge (2 mins)

"Manhood is about being present, not perfect." –Phil Black

Session 4 Post Assessment

1. What does it mean to be "at-risk"?

2. List examples of at-risk behaviors.

3. What are short and long term consequences of engaging in at-risk behaviors?

"Manhood is about being present, not perfect." –Phil Black

SESSION 5: My Image and I

Unit 1 S5: Session Objectives

By the end of this session the learner will be able to:

1. List personal behaviors that they would like to change.

2. Acknowledge how others view them.

3. Explain the difference between a person's self-image and reputation.

4. Identify ways to build a good reputation and maintain a positive self-image.

AGENDA

1. Sign-in

2. Snack & Chat

3. Welcome

4. Review

5. Pre Assessment

6. Warm-up

7. Session Introduction
   - ❑ Overview
   - ❑ Objectives
   - ❑ Agenda

8. Lesson
   - ❑ What would they say?
   - ❑ Define Terms
   - ❑ Discussion

9. Close
   - ❑ Post-Assessment
   - ❑ Clean-up
   - ❑ Reflection
   - ❑ Announcements
   - ❑ Parting Pledge

"Manhood is about being present, not perfect." –Phil Black

43

ACTIVITIES
1. Review: Active Knowledge Sharing 2. Warm-Up: Change 3. Game: Airplane Darts 4. What would they say?

ROOM SET-UP	MATERIALS NEEDED
Full or Half Circle Seating	1. Session 5 Review Worksheet 2. Writing paper 3. Flipchart Paper 4. Dry Erase Board 5. Markers 6. Pens

SESSION PREP

1. Ensure sign-in sheet is ready.

2. Print Pre and Post assessments.

3. Set-up transition music.

4. Make sure snack are ready for distribution.

5. Draw a large bull's eye for the Airplane Darts Game.

6. *Write* and post: Objectives, Agenda, and Review Questions on separate sheets of flipchart paper. *If Dry Erase Board is available, use it to write session objectives. Reserve flipchart for the other information.*

7. On a separate flipchart write:
   - ❏ Parents
   - ❏ Siblings/cousins
   - ❏ Best friend
   - ❏ Teacher
   - ❏ Principal
   - ❏ Others

Draw a line down the middle of each sheet. Below the title, to the left of the line write "Best." To the right of the line write "Change."

"Manhood is about being present, not perfect." –Phil Black

UNIT 1 S5: SESSION DETAILS		
1.5 - 2 hr		
	Pre-Session	Set up all materials and music.
3 mins	**Sign-in**	Have students sign in as they enter the designated space.
8 mins	**Snack & Chat**	
3 mins	**Welcome**	Thank students for coming and introduce the warm-up
(optional)	**Highlights and Do-Overs**	
6 mins	**Warm-up: Change**	Airplane Darts 1. Have students make an airplane using print paper. 2. *Tell* them: The objective is to see who can make the best airplane dart. 3. Once everyone has designed a plane, have them take turns throwing it at the large bull's eye constructed during session prep. 4. Allow each person 1-2 throws.
3 mins	**Session Introduction**	1. Overview: Today we are going to discuss you and your image. Specifically, how you see yourself and how others view you. 2. Objectives: Have a volunteer read the objectives. Provide any clarity you feel is needed. 3. Agenda: After the objectives have been covered, reveal, and recite the agenda.
25 mins	**Lesson**	Activity: "What would they say?" *Explain*: This is called: "What would they say?" Sitting around the room are many different people. On each sheet, list what that person would describe as your best quality as well as something you need to improve upon. *After students are done, have them share the answers listed.* 1. Explain the difference between self-image (how we see ourselves) and our reputation (how others see us).

"Manhood is about being present, not perfect." –Phil Black

		Note to students: Our self-image can be affected by our reputation. Have someone explain how.
		
		2. As a group, identify key ways to build a good reputation:
		    ❑ Treat people nice
		    ❑ Keep your word
		    ❑ Behave
		    ❑ Be respectful, etc.

6 mins	**Break**	
19 mins	**Close**	Post-Assessment: Have students complete the post assessment. (6 mins) Clean-up (3 mins) Reflection: What is something that you will do over the next week to build a good reputation? (6 mins) Announcements (2 mins) Parting Pledge (2 mins)

"Manhood is about being present, not perfect." –Phil Black

46

Session 5 Post Assessment

1. What is self-image?

2. What is a reputation?

3. What is the difference between self-image and reputation?

4. Explain what it means to have a positive or healthy self-image?

5. How does a person's self-image possibly affect their self-image? How can a negative reputation impact your self-image?

"Manhood is about being present, not perfect." –Phil Black

SESSION 6: My Image and I (part II)

Unit 1   S6: Session Objectives

By the end of this session the learner will be able to:

1. Recognize how the perception of others can affect our reputation.

2. Explain the difference between a person's self-image and their reputation.

3. Determine which factors help to build one's self-image and reputation.

4. Acknowledge how others see them.

AGENDA

1. Sign-in

2. Snack & Chat

3. Welcome

4. Warm-up & Discussion

5. Session Introduction
   - ❏ Overview
   - ❏ Objectives
   - ❏ Agenda

6. Lesson
   - ❏ Define Terms
   - ❏ What would they say?
   - ❏ Building Self-Image and Reputation

7. Close
   - ❏ Post-Assessment
   - ❏ Clean-up
   - ❏ Reflection
   - ❏ Announcements
   - ❏ Parting Pledge

"Manhood is about being present, not perfect." –Phil Black

ACTIVITIES
1. Warm up: Two Truths and a Lie 2. Building Self-Image and Reputation

ROOM SET-UP	MATERIALS NEEDED
Full or Half Circle Seating	1. Worksheets (Scenarios) 2. Flipchart Paper 3. Post-Its 4. Dry Erase 5. Markers 6. Pens

SESSION PREP

1. Ensure sign-in sheet is ready.

2. Print:
   - ❏ Post assessments
   - ❏ Copies of the profile sheets

3. Set-up transition music.

4. Make sure snacks are ready for distribution.

5. Write and post: Objectives and Agenda on separate sheets of flipchart paper. *If Dry Erase Board is available, use it to write session objectives. Reserve flipchart for the other information.*

"Manhood is about being present, not perfect." –Phil Black

SESSION DETAILS		
1.5 - 2 hr		
	Pre-Session	Set up all materials and music.
3 mins	**Sign-in**	Have students sign in as they enter the designated space.
15 mins	**Snack & Chat**	
3 mins	**Welcome**	Thank students for coming and introduce the warm-up
12 mins	**Warm up: Two Truths and a Lie**	1. Hand each student a post-it note 2. Each student must write two statements that are true about themselves and one statement that is a lie. 3. The lie must be written in a way to appear truthful. 4. After everyone has written their answers, have each student share their answers with the group. While sharing, the each group member gets one opportunity to guess which statement is false.
(optional)	**Highlights and Do-Overs**	
1-3 mins	**Session Intro**	Today we are going to build on last week's session regarding Reputation and Self-Image. Before we look at two different character profiles, we'll do a quick review.
3 - 5 mins	**Review**	Review questions: 1. What is a reputation? 2. What is self-image? 3. How do you build your reputation and self-image?
30 mins	**Lesson**	1. Pass out the worksheet: Nick's Character profile. 2. Read the directions aloud and ask for volunteers to read each role. 3. At the conclusion, answer the questions as a group.

"Manhood is about being present, not perfect." –Phil Black

		Repeat the process for Gerald's profile. You may mix things up by having students work alone, silently, in pairs or small group.

19 mins	**Close**	Post-Assessment: Have students complete the post assessment. (6 mins)
		
		Clean-up (3 mins)
		
		Reflection:
		   ❑ What questions have today's session raised about your own reputation?
		   ❑ How do you anticipate these questions affecting your future decisions? (6 mins)
		
		Announcements (2 mins)
		
		Parting Pledge (2 mins)

"Manhood is about being present, not perfect." –Phil Black

Session 6 Worksheet Activity

Building the Best Me

 Nick is a 17 year old senior at Clark High School. Nick's first three years at Clark did not go very well. We've briefly interviewed five people who regularly interact with Nick. Read their comments and answer the questions at the end. Be prepared to discuss your answers with the group.

Tonya (Nick's Mom): I don't know what to do with Nick. He talks back, stays out all night, and never does anything to help around the house. He is going to turn eighteen in a few months, I don't know if he is going to graduate and attend college- but he can't live here forever.

Cook (Nick's former basketball Coach): Nick is an amazing athlete! I have never seen such raw talent on the court, but his attitude is so bad that I couldn't afford to have him on the team. Nick always came to practice late or high on drugs. Some of the other players started following his lead- not to mention: keeping him eligible was a weekly task. I had to cut him.

Keisha (Nick's ex-girlfriend): I still like Nick, but we can't go together anymore. He tries talking to too many other girls. Plus, we are seniors now and I don't know what direction he is going in. I don't want to be with somebody who just wants to smoke weed and play video games every day. I'm trying to better myself.

Mr. Bates (Nick's Principal): Nick is a good kid, but I am concerned about where he is going to end up. I've already had to suspend him on four occasions. The last time, a teacher reported that he smelled like pot. When Nick arrived at my office, he appeared high as a kite. I'm just not sure if he's going to make it.

Will (Nick's Best Friend): Nickel (bag)? That's my dude. Sometimes we leave after third hour to go smoke one. He always down. I'm just glad he not tryin' to hoop no more. When he was on the team I didn't have nobody to hang wit'.

Discussion Questions:

1. If you were a business owner, or college recruiter sent to evaluate Nick, what would be your impression of him based on the above interviews?

2. What is your first impression of Will?

3. Where do you see Nick in 3 to 5 years? Explain.

"Manhood is about being present, not perfect." –Phil Black

Session 6 Worksheet Activity 2[1]

Building the Best Me II

 Gerald is a fifteen year old sophomore at Hampton Leadership Academy. We've briefly interviewed five people who regularly interact with Gerald. Read their comments and answer the questions at the end. Be prepared to discuss your answers within the group.

Erica (Gerald's Mom): Gerald isn't perfect, but he is a good kid. I sometimes have to get on him about cleaning his room, but for the most part, he helps me out around the house. I normally get home from work around 6:30 PM, so he makes sure his sister and brother have completed their homework and have snacks after school.

Coach Banks (Gerald's Football Coach): Gerald has gotten much better since last season. I would certainly say it is due to his hard work. Immediately after the season, he asked for honest feedback on his performance and I told him that he needs to get stronger, and he has to show more leadership. Since then, Gerald has come to the weight room after school three times per week. I have also noticed him encouraging others to show up as well. During spring practice he is usually first in line for drills, and often steps up to demonstrate different techniques.

Krystal (Gerald's girlfriend): I really like Gerald. He thinks it is because he is so cute, which he is, but I am more impressed with how he carries himself. Gerald doesn't follow the crowd, and even though we might argue sometimes, he never says things to intentionally hurt my feelings.

Mrs. Chambers (Gerald's English Teacher): Gerald has come a long way. When the semester first began, I could tell that he was very insecure about his reading and writing skills. One day after class, he asked if I would be willing to tutor him once per week. After the first month, I realized he was getting much better. Turns out, Gerald was doing extra work on his own- outside of our tutoring sessions.

Jay (Gerald's Best Friend): Gee is funny. He is always making people laugh. He doesn't know it, but I really look up to him. Seeing how strong he got over the summer, and how much better he is doing in school, has made me want step up.

Discussion Questions:

1. What words would you use to describe Gerald based on these comments?

2. Would you be open to hanging out with Gerald? Why or why not?

---

[1] This activity was created from a similar one featured in: Social Skills Activities for Secondary Students by Darlene Mannix

"Manhood is about being present, not perfect." –Phil Black

3. If someone else made a negative comment about Gerald, are you more or less likely to believe it (based on what you have learned about him)?

"Manhood is about being present, not perfect." –Phil Black

Session 6 Post Assessment

1. What factors help to build a person's self-image and reputation?

2. How can your life be affected by people's perception of you?

3. What have you learned by evaluating both Nick and Gerald?

4. What are ways you can begin to improve your self-image and reputation?

"Manhood is about being present, not perfect." –Phil Black

SESSION 7: Unit 1 Review

Session Objectives

By the end of this session the learner will be able to:

1. Identify the most impactful aspects of Unit I.

2. Share any changes made since the first session.

3. Recognize other students that have made improvements.

4. Set goals for the next unit.

AGENDA

1. Sign-in

2. Snack & Chat

3. Welcome

4. Warm-up

5. Pre Assessment (optional)

6. Session Introduction
   - ❑ Overview
   - ❑ Objectives
   - ❑ Agenda

7. Lesson
   - ❑ Activity
   - ❑ Recap
   - ❑ Norms
   - ❑ Expectations

8. Close
   - ❑ Clean-up
   - ❑ Reflection
   - ❑ Announcements
   - ❑ Parting Pledge

"Manhood is about being present, not perfect." –Phil Black

ACTIVITIES

1. Warm-up: What I've learned
2. Teach me

ROOM SET-UP	MATERIALS NEEDED
Full or Half Circle Seating	1. Flipchart Paper 2. Dry Erase Board 3. Printing Paper 4. Markers 5. Pens

SESSION PREP

1. Ensure sign-in sheet is ready.

2. Print:
   - ❑ Pre and post assessments
   - ❑ Copies of opening and closing pledge

3. Set-up transition music.

4. Make sure snacks are ready to distribute.

5. *Write* and post: Objectives, Agenda, Norms & Expectations, and Review Questions on separate sheets of flipchart paper. *If Dry Erase Board is available, use it to write session objectives. Reserve flipchart for the other information.*

6. On a full sheet of flipchart, write an example of a group presentation/teach back outline:
   - ❑ Name: (Write your name as the example)
   - ❑ Objective: To share what I've learned from this group since we have started.
   - ❑ Main Points:

     ➢Point #1: (List something you have learned about them as a group)

     ➢Point #2:

     ➢Point #3:

"Manhood is about being present, not perfect." –Phil Black

SESSION DETAILS		
1.5 - 2 hr		
	Pre-Session	Set up all materials and music.
3 mins	**Sign-in**	Have students sign in as they enter the designated space.
15 mins	**Snack & Chat**	
3 mins	**Welcome**	Thank students for coming and introduce the warm-up
5-8 mins	**Warm-up: What I've Learned**	1. Supply each student with a pen and paper. 2. Have them record a list of everything that they have learned throughout the unit. *Note: Directions for this can be very loose, as the goal is to see what students have been able to retain on their own.* Once complete, instruct them not to share their results, until given further instructions.
(optional)	**Highlights and Do-Overs**	
5 mins	**Break**	
	Session Introduction	1. Overview: Today we are going review the entire unit, and recap all that you have learned. 2. Objectives: Have a volunteer read the objectives. Provide any clarity you feel is necessary. 3. Agenda: After the objectives have been covered, reveal, and recite the agenda.
45 mins	**Lesson**	<u>Activity: Teach me</u> *Explain*: Rather than completing our normal review, where you answer various questions, you will lead the group by teaching me what you've learned. 1. Separate the larger group into equal smaller groups of 3-5.

"Manhood is about being present, not perfect." –Phil Black

		2. Using their combined written responses, have them compare notes, and come to a consensus of what information is correct.
		3. Give each group 15-20 minutes to determine how they would like to present what they've learned.
		Examples: Skit, Commercial, Activity, Drawing, a Rap, etc.
		Each group has 2-3 minutes to present their lesson.
		Presentations
25 mins	**Close**	Post-Assessment: Have students complete the post assessment. (6 mins)
		Clean-up (4 mins)
		Reflection: What are you most confident about after doing this review session? (10 mins)
		Announcements (2 mins)
		Parting Pledge (2 mins)

"Manhood is about being present, not perfect." –Phil Black

SESSION 8: Assessment, Recognition, and Reflection

Unit 1 S8: Session Objectives

By the end of this session the learner will be able to:

1. Identify the most impactful aspects of Unit I.

2. Share any changes they've made since their first session.

3. Recognize other students that have made improvements.

4. Set goals for the next unit.

AGENDA

1. Sign-in

2. Snack & Chat

3. Welcome

4. Q & A

5. Unit Assessment

6. Reactions

7. Recognition

8. Reflection

9. Unit II Overview

10. Close
    - Clean-up
    - Announcements
    - Parting Pledge

"Manhood is about being present, not perfect." –Phil Black

ACTIVITIES

1. Unit Assessment
2. Games

ROOM SET-UP	MATERIALS NEEDED
Full or Half Circle Seating	1. Unit Assessment 2. Certificates or awards (Unit I Completion, Most Improved, and Man of the Month). 3. Games 4. Art materials 5. Dry Erase Board 6. Markers 7. Pens

SESSION PREP

1. Ensure sign-in sheet is ready.

2. Print Unit Assessments.

3. Set-up transition music.

4. Purchase special meal to celebrate.

"Manhood is about being present, not perfect." –Phil Black

SESSION DETAILS		
1.5 - 2 hr		
	Pre-Session	Set up all materials and music.
3 mins	**Sign-in**	Have students sign in as they enter the designated space.
8 mins	**Snack & Chat**	
3 mins	**Welcome**	
(optional)	**Highlights and Do-Overs**	
20 mins	**Recognition**	Share words of encouragement, while recognizing each individual, and their personal progress.
30+ mins	**Lesson**	The remaining time should be used as free play/team building. Best Practices ❑ Special Snacks/food (e.g. cup cakes, sub platter, etc.) ❑ Board Games ❑ Video Games ❑ Drawing materials ❑ Open gym
3 mins	**Reflection**	What part of Unit I has made the most impact on you? What personal changes have you made since the beginning of this program?
8 mins	**Unit II Overview**	Provide a brief overview of what the next unit will cover.
5 mins	**Break**	
25 mins	**Close**	Clean-up (4 mins) Announcements (2 mins) Parting Pledge (2 mins)

"Manhood is about being present, not perfect." –Phil Black

Unit 1 Assessment

1. The Manhood Project is a _____ and _____
   development program.

2. The Motto of The Manhood Project is, "You don't have to be _____
   but you do have to be _____."

3. The Five Virtues of Manhood are:
   1. _____
   2. _____
   3. _____
   4. _____
   5. _____

4. List the TMP Norms
   1. _____   7. _____
   2. _____   8. _____
   3. _____   9. _____
   4. _____   10. _____
   5. _____   11. _____
   6. _____

5. Describe the type of man you want to be viewed as.

6. What are potential consequences to at-risk behaviors?

"Manhood is about being present, not perfect." –Phil Black

63

7. What is the difference between self-image and reputation?

8. What are several ways to build a healthy self-image?

9. How can you build a positive reputation?

10. What lesson stands out to you the most? Explain why.

"Manhood is about being present, not perfect." –Phil Black

SPECIAL SESSION: Locker Room

For Locker Room Lesson template, visit the Resource section

"Manhood is about being present, not perfect." –Phil Black

Unit 2: Communication

"I learned that courage was not the absence of fear, but the triumph over it. The brave man is not he who does not feel afraid, but he who conquers that fear."

-Nelson Mandela

"Manhood is about being present, not perfect." –Phil Black

Unit 2 Background and Overview

This next unit focuses on **communication**. Communication extends beyond the words we use to express our thoughts, and feelings. Communication can include body language, the vehicles we use to communicate, and who we communicate with. Often, we fail to reflect on our behavior when we communicate with others; we simply just do it without realizing the many different facets associated with positive communication. This unit allows participants to study, reflect, and improve their communication skills that will aide them in fostering better relationships and personal outcomes.

Understanding how to communicate in a healthy way is an essential building block. We address communication early in the curriculum because is it often the key to unlocking other healthy behaviors, and addressing (and improving or removing) past unhealthy behaviors. Our study of communication addresses expression in multiple forms.

SESSIONS included in this unit:

SESSION 09: Guest Speaker
SESSION 10: Student 1:1s and Self Care Day
SESSION 11: Communication 101 - Defining Communication
SESSION 12: Communication 102 - Environments and Individuals
SESSION 13: Communication and Technology
SESSION 14: Understanding Communicative Spaces
SESSION 15: Reputation Impact
SESSION 16: Unit Assessment, Reflection, and Recognition

"Manhood is about being present, not perfect." –Phil Black

Lesson Plans + Materials

SESSION 9: Guest Speaker

For Guest Speaker Lesson template, please visit the Resource section

"Manhood is about being present, not perfect." –Phil Black

SESSION 10: Student One-on-Ones

For One-on-One Lesson template, please visit the Resource section

"Manhood is about being present, not perfect." –Phil Black

SESSION 11: Communication 101 Defining Communication

Unit 2   S11: Session Objectives

By the end of this session the learner will be able to:

1. Define Communication.

2. There are two main types of communication (verbal and nonverbal). List an example of both.

3. Explain what is meant by the phrase: "You are *always* communicating."

4. Express the importance of being aware of your communication.

AGENDA

1. Sign-in

2. Snack & Chat

3. Welcome

4. Warm-up

5. Pre Assessment (optional)

6. Session Introduction
   - ❏ Overview
   - ❏ Objectives
   - ❏ Agenda

7. Lesson
   - ❏ Activity
   - ❏ Recap
   - ❏ Norms
   - ❏ Expectations

8. Close
   - ❏ Post-Assessment
   - ❏ Clean up
   - ❏ Reflection
   - ❏ Announcements
   - ❏ Parting Pledge

"Manhood is about being present, not perfect." –Phil Black

ACTIVITIES

1. Taboo
2. Guesstures

ROOM SET-UP	MATERIALS NEEDED
Full or Half Circle Seating	1. Flipchart Paper 2. Dry Erase Board 3. Printing Paper 4. Markers 5. Pens 6. Taboo (Board Game) 7. Guesstures (Board Game) 8. Extra treats (e.g. Chocolate bars or fruit candy) as prizes for game winners.

SESSION PREP

1. Ensure sign-in sheet is ready.

2. Print:

   ❑ Pre and post assessments

3. Set-up transition music.

4. Make sure snacks are ready for distribution.

5. Write and post: Objectives, Agenda, Norms & Expectations, and Review Questions on separate sheets of flipchart paper. *If Dry Erase Board is available, use it to write session objectives. Reserve flipchart for the other information.*

6. Write on flipchart Paper the following definition and pie graph.

   ❑ Communication: The process of giving, receiving, or exchanging of information.
   ❑ Pie graph: Verbal 10% and Nonverbal 90%.

SESSION DETAILS		
1.5 - 2 hr		
	Pre-Session	Set up all materials and music. *Note: flipchart with definition and graph should be covered in some way until it is time to discuss.*
3 mins	**Sign-in**	Have students sign in as they enter the designated space.
15 mins	**Snack & Chat**	
3 mins	**Welcome**	Thank students for coming and introduce the warm-up. *Say*: We are going to play a game. How many of you have ever played the game Taboo? (Observe responses and take mental note of the results). Today, we'll play a few rounds of Taboo as our warm-up. **Before explaining the rules and beginning the activity, you may ask for H&Ds or do a short review. If you choose not to, simply go right into the activity.*
(optional)	**Highlights and Do-Overs**	
	Review	
10 mins	**Warm-up: Taboo**	1. Have students count off by two's in order to divide them into two separate teams. 2. Explain the objective of the Taboo game (which is to get your team to say the bolded word at the top of the card, without saying any of the five beneath it or using body motions nor sounds). 3. Each person gets:45 seconds to describe as many words as they can.
6 mins	**Reflection/ Discussion**	1. What did you find easy about playing this game? 2. How was the game difficult? 3. Who can share a time when they said something, but the other person misunderstood what you were trying to say?

"Manhood is about being present, not perfect." –Phil Black

	Session Introduction	Today we are going to discuss communication. What exactly is communication? ❏ Take and record the various responses on flipchart or dry erase. ❏ Once you have taken at least three responses, reveal the pre-written definition. Main Point: Communication occurs when a sender expresses an emotion or a feeling. Communication can be received, given, or exchanged. *To ensure understanding, you may ask for examples.* The warm-up activity demonstrated one way that communication occurs. After our break, we will visit the second form of communication.
	Break	
10 mins	**Session Continued**	Next, we'll play a game called Guesstures. ❏ Explain the rules of the game: you have to get your team to guess the words featured on the card through body language and motion. ❏ No words or sounds can be used during this game. ❏ Play 2-3 rounds. Reflection 1. Was this game more difficult or easier than Taboo? 2. For those participants guessing, which game was easier to understand (the game using words, or the game using actions)? Why?
25 mins	**Lesson**	There are two types of communication- verbal and nonverbal. We express ourselves through the words we say, but we also communicate our thoughts and feelings with our actions. Give examples: -A person with his head on a desk could be communicating what? If someone is smiling they could be communicating what? -If f I ask a question and no one responds, what might that suggest to me?

"Manhood is about being present, not perfect." –Phil Black

		*Reveal the Pie Graph Main Point: The reason most people find the second game to be easier, is because most of our communication is nonverbal. If I look at you with a frown on my face, I don't have to tell you that I am what? (*Upset*) Why is it important to be aware of what you are saying to people verbally? (*Target answer: To reduce the chances of offending someone or being misunderstood*). In like manner, we also have to be well aware of our nonverbal communication (or body language). There is a saying: "You are always communicating." Someone tell us what that means. (*Target answer: No matter what, we are always expressing something to others.*)
15 mins	**Close**	Post-Assessment: Have students complete post assessment (6 mins) Clean-up (4 mins) Announcements (2 mins) Parting Pledge (2 mins)

"Manhood is about being present, not perfect." –Phil Black

Session 11 Post Assessment

1. What is communication?

2. What are the two types of communication?

3. Why is it important to be aware of what and how you are communicating to others?

SESSION 12: Communication 102 - Environments and Individuals

Unit 2   S12: Session Objectives

By the end of this session the learner will be able to:

1. Discuss what it feels like to be in an unfamiliar environment.

2. Identify specific behaviors or elements that cause them to be uncomfortable in new spaces.

3. Share methods used to overcome any insecurities or anxieties, often felt when adapting to a new environment or person.

4. Communicate the importance of being aware of the spaces we occupy.

AGENDA

1. Sign-in

2. Snack & Chat

3. Welcome

4. Warm-up

5. Pre Assessment (optional)

6. Session Introduction
    - Overview
    - Objectives
    - Agenda

7. Lesson
    - Define terms
    - What would they say?
    - Building Self-Image and Reputation

8. Close
    - Post-Assessment
    - Clean-up
    - Reflection
    - Announcements
    - Parting Pledge

"Manhood is about being present, not perfect." –Phil Black

ACTIVITIES
1. Pair Share (Review) 2. Where am I?

ROOM SET-UP	MATERIALS NEEDED
Full or Half Circle Seating	1. Review Questions for Communication 101 2. Flipchart Paper 3. Dry Erase Markers 4. Pens

SESSION PREP

1. Ensure sign-in sheet is available and ready.

2. Print:
   - Post assessments

3. Write: Review Questions on the board

4. Set-up transition music.

5. Make sure snacks are ready for distribution.

6. Write and post: Objectives and Agenda on separate sheets of flipchart paper. *If Dry Erase Board is available, use it to write session objectives. Reserve flipchart for the other information.*

7. Print worksheets.

8. YouTube video "*New Kid*:"
   https://youtu.be/FdeioVndUhs

SESSION DETAILS		
1.5 - 2 hr		
	Pre-Session	Set up all materials and music.
3 mins	**Sign-in**	Have students sign in as they enter the designated space.
15 mins	**Snack & Chat**	
3 mins	**Welcome**	Thank students for coming and introduce the warm-up
(optional)	**Highlights and Do-Overs**	
7 mins	**Review: Pair Share**	1. Have students select a partner. 2. Assign one review question to each pair, then have them share their answers with the entire group.

25 mins	**Warm-up: *New Kid* (YouTube Video)**	1. Play the Video: *New Kid* (12 mins)
		
		2. Facilitate a brief discussion about the film. (13 mins)
		
		    ☐ Explain. How did this movie make you feel? Why?
		
		    ☐ What was different about the environment Joseph originally came from in comparison to his current one?
		
		    ☐ What do you think was going through Joseph's mind when he had to stand in front of the class?
		
		    ☐ How did Joseph's current behavior differ from the behavior in his old school?

5 mins	**Break**	
3 - 4 mins	**Session Introduction**	1. Overview: To build on last week's lesson, we'll begin discussing what it's like to communicate in different environments. Specifically, environments that are within unfamiliar territory. 2. Objectives: Have a volunteer read the objectives. *Provide any clarity you feel is needed.*

"Manhood is about being present, not perfect." –Phil Black

21 mins	**Lesson**	1. With the same partner, have students discuss a time in their life, when they were in a new environment for the first time and initially felt uncomfortable. Have them identify specific details about the environment or individuals present that made them feel uncomfortable.
		
		*Give 6 minutes (3 minutes per student) for sharing their answers. Then have 4-6 volunteers share with the group.
		
		Questions to consider:
		
		    ☐ Where were you?
		    ☐ Why were you there?
		    ☐ What made you uncomfortable?
		    ☐ What helped you to feel more at ease?
		
		2. Ask/List:
		
		    ☐ Was it the environment or certain people that made you feel uncomfortable? *(Record the number of responses for both categories).*
		
		    ☐ Be specific and detail exactly what made you feel that way about that particular environment or person.
		
		    ☐ How did you become comfortable? (Or did you just leave)?

5 mins	**Break**	
20 mins	**Close**	Post-Assessment: Have students complete post assessment (6 mins) Clean-up (3 mins) Reflection: (5 mins) When thinking about your experience, how can you relate to Joseph in the video? *After everyone has shared, ask:* What do you think the main point of this lesson was? *Target answer: To help us better understand how we can make others feel welcomed or unwelcomed in an environment based on:*

| | | (1) how we treat them directly or (2) what they observe from us through our behavior.

Announcements (2 mins)

Parting Pledge (2 mins) |
| --- | --- | --- |

"Manhood is about being present, not perfect." –Phil Black

Session 12 Post Assessment

1. What makes a person uncomfortable in a new environment?

2. What are ways to make people comfortable?

3. How can you overcome being uncomfortable in a new space?

4. Why is it important to be aware of the space that you are in?

"Manhood is about being present, not perfect." –Phil Black

SESSION 13: Communication and Technology

Unit 2   S13: Session Objectives

By the end of this session the learner will be able to:

1. Debate their views regarding privacy and social media.

2. Express why the internet and other technologies are considered public spaces.

3. Determine what is considered appropriate communication over technology.

4. Recognize how cyber communication can affect their futures.

AGENDA

1. Sign-in

2. Snack & Chat

3. Welcome

4. Pre Assessment

5. Session Introduction
   - ❏ Overview
   - ❏ Objectives
   - ❏ Agenda

6. Warm-up

7. Lesson
   - ❏ Open space
   - ❏ Discussion
   - ❏ Digital Footprint

8. Close
   - ❏ Post-Assessment
   - ❏ Clean-up
   - ❏ Reflection
   - ❏ Announcements
   - ❏ Parting Pledge

"Manhood is about being present, not perfect." –Phil Black

ACTIVITIES
1. Review: Active Knowledge Sharing 2. Warm-Up: Snap Debate 3. Open Space Technology 4. Case Study

ROOM SET-UP	MATERIALS NEEDED
Full or Half Circle Seating	1. Session 12 Review Worksheet 2. Writing paper 3. Flipchart Paper 4. Internet Stories 5. Dry Erase Board 6. Markers 7. Pens

SESSION PREP

1. Ensure sign-in sheet is ready.

2. Print pre and post assessments.

3. Set-up transition music.

4. Make sure snacks are ready for distribution.

5. *Write* and post: Objectives and Agenda on separate sheets of flipchart paper.
   If Dry Erase Board is available, use it to write session objectives. Reserve flipchart for the other information.

6. On separate flipchart paper, write two stories about the following (with regards to technology):
   - Bullying
   - Job loss
   - Expulsion

7. Print copies of the Yuri Wright Story: http://www.theblaze.com/stories/2012/01/23/catholic-high-school-football-star-expelled-loses-scholarship-over-racist-sexual-tweets/

"Manhood is about being present, not perfect." –Phil Black

SESSION DETAILS		
1.5 - 2 hr		
	Pre-Session	Set up all materials and music.
3 mins	**Sign-in**	Have students sign in as they enter the designated space.
8 mins	**Snack & Chat**	
3 mins	**Welcome**	Thank students for coming and introduce the warm-up
(optional)	**Highlights and Do-Overs**	
	Review	(1) Have students individually complete the Session 12 Review sheet. (2) After they have answered as many questions as they can, allow them to walk around the room and compare answers. (3) Students are allowed to change answers if they would like. (4) At the end of the share, go over the worksheet with the entire group.
6 mins	**Pre Assessment**	
8 mins	**Warm-up: Snap Debate**	*Explain*: Today's session will begin with a quick debate. I'll read a statement. If you agree with that statement, stand to my left. If you disagree, stand to my right. 1. *Read* the statement: My Twitter, Instagram, and Facebook pages are my business and I should be able to post whatever I want. 2. Now separate the two groups (agree/disagree). If they are unequal, ask for volunteers to assist in leveling the groups. 3. Have both teams select 1-2 spokes persons. 4. Give the students five minutes to come up with their pro/con arguments regarding the statement. 5. Once time is up, have them debate their positions.

"Manhood is about being present, not perfect." –Phil Black

		*At the end *explain*: Internet privacy is a hot debate topic. As the world continues to grow and become more dependent, the rules for communicating on the internet and through technology in general- are becoming more defined. With that said, it is important to be aware of the potential dangers that come with internet privacy and communication.
5 mins	**Session Introduction**	1. Overview: Today we are going to talk about communication and technology. 2. Objectives: Have a volunteer read the objectives. *Provide any clarity you feel is needed.* 3. Agenda: After the objectives have been covered, reveal and recite the agenda.
20 mins	**Lesson**	<u>Activity I: Open Space Exercise</u> *Explain*: Located around the room are multiple stories about people and their communication over technology. We are going to give you 15 minutes to review them, then we'll have a discussion. *After students are done, have them share their reactions.* Guided questions 1. Which story stood out to you the most and why?
4 mins	**Break**	
20 mins	**Lesson (cont'd)**	<u>Activity II: Case Study</u> 1. Hand out copies of the Yuri story. 2. Designate ten minutes for students to read the article. 3. Discuss student reactions. Guided Questions 1. Why do you think Yuri continued to write the tweets after being warned? 2. Do you feel that this could affect Yuri's future? Explain. *Define digital footprint and discuss the importance of showing discretion.*

"Manhood is about being present, not perfect." –Phil Black

3 mins	**Break**	
25 mins	**Close**	Post-Assessment: Have students complete the post assessment. (6 mins) Clean-up (4 mins) Reflection: How has this session affected the way you see social media and other forms of cyber communication? (10 mins) Announcements (2 mins) Parting Pledge (2 mins)

"Manhood is about being present, not perfect." –Phil Black

Session 13 Review

1. To impart information means the same as:
    a. guess
    b. hold
    c. give
    d. none of these

2. To exchange information means the same as:
    a. share
    b. take
    c. forget
    d. none of these

3. To infer means to assume. T or F

4. In communication, our words mean more than our body language. T or F

5. What does: "We are always communicating" mean?

6. What is the difference between public and private?

7. List three examples of each (public and private spaces).

8. What makes a conversation or action inappropriate?

Session 13 Post Assessment

1. What makes the internet a public space?

2. How could a comment you would normally make to a friend in verbal form, be seen as inappropriate when made in written form over social media? Give an example.

3. How could your use of profane or vulgar communication over social media, affect your future?

"Manhood is about being present, not perfect." –Phil Black

SESSION 14: Understanding Communicative Spaces

Session Objectives
By the end of this session the learner will be able to:

1. Recognize the different communicative spaces (e.g. home, school, work).

2. Discuss how our communication changes based on our environment.

3. Identify the difference between public and private interactions.

4. Express why our language and behavior should match our environment.

AGENDA

1. Sign-in

2. Snacks & Chat

3. Welcome

4. Warm-up

5. Pre Assessment (optional)

6. Session Introduction
    - ❑ Overview
    - ❑ Objectives
    - ❑ Agenda

7. Lesson
    - ❑ Activity
    - ❑ Recap
    - ❑ Norms
    - ❑ Expectations

8. Close
    - ❑ Clean-up
    - ❑ Reflection
    - ❑ Announcements
    - ❑ Parting Pledge

"Manhood is about being present, not perfect." –Phil Black

ACTIVITIES

ROOM SET-UP	MATERIALS NEEDED
Full or Half Circle Seating	1. Flipchart Paper 2. Dry Erase Board 3. Printing Paper 4. Markers 5. Pens

SESSION PREP

1. Ensure sign-in sheet is ready.

2. Print:
   - ❏ Pre and post assessments
   - ❏ Copies of opening and closing pledge

3. Set-up transition music.

4. Make sure snacks are ready to distribute.

5. *Write* and post: Objectives, Agenda, Norms & Expectations, and Review Questions on separate sheets of flipchart paper. *If Dry Erase Board is available, use it to write session objectives. Reserve flipchart for the other information.*

"Manhood is about being present, not perfect." –Phil Black

SESSION DETAILS		
1.5 - 2 hr		
	Pre-Session	Set up all materials and music.
3 mins	**Sign-in**	Have students sign in as they enter the designated space.
15 mins	**Snack & Chat**	
3 mins	**Welcome**	Thank students for coming and introduce the warm-up
(optional)	**Highlights and Do-Overs**	
	Review	
8 mins	**Warm-up**	
6 mins	**Pre Assessment**	
	Session Introduction	

25 mins	**Lesson**	Activity I: Review
		
		1. Using flipchart (half sheets) write a review question that corresponds with the objectives from the last session.
		
		2. Have students choose a partner and provide each pair with a question to answer.
		
		3. Once each pair has completed a question, review all answers with the entire group.
		
		4. *Ask*:
		  a. How have you used this information in the past week?
		
		  b. What have you noticed about your communication and the communication of others?
		
		  c. What adjustments, if any, did you find yourself making when talking to others?

	Break	

"Manhood is about being present, not perfect." –Phil Black

	Lesson (cont'd)	Activity II: Communication Spaces 1. *Write* various communicative spaces onto individual (half sheets) flipchart (e.g. Home, Mall, School). 2. Have students gather into groups of 3 or 4. 3. Step one: Identify if the designated space public (open to anyone, person, or group of people) or private (designated for specific individuals or groups). (2 minutes) 4. Step two: List the types of individuals or groups of people, you may encounter in the given spaces. (6 minutes) 5. Step three: Discuss/list the types of conversation topics you would *not* have in those spaces (restrictions). (7 minutes) *Example:* Communicative Space: Home Type of Space: Private People: Mom, Dad, siblings, Uncle etc. Conversation Topics: no restrictions Discussion Questions 1. What is the difference between Public and Private? *Have the formal definitions available.* 2. What spaces have more restrictions- public or private, and why? 3. When engaging in private conversations in public spaces, what potential problems could arise? 4. How should our environment affect the types of conversations we have? 5. How does your "private socially-appropriate" conversation become inappropriate depending on who is present? *Major point: Appropriate conversations, behaviors or overall communication becomes inappropriate depending upon your location and*

"Manhood is about being present, not perfect." –Phil Black

		the individuals present.
		6. What are some ways to avoid being viewed as inappropriate?
	Break	
25 mins	**Close**	Post-Assessment: Have students complete the post assessment. (6 mins) Clean-up (4 mins) Reflection (10 mins) Announcements (2 mins) Parting Pledge (2 mins)

SESSION 15: Reputation Impact

Unit 2   S15: Session Objectives

By the end of this session the learner will be able to:

1. Share how individuals/schools make decisions based on facts and information, rather than emotional connections.

2. Assess how a person's personal life and other factors can influence their business decisions.

3. Discuss how patterns of behavior, lead to lasting impressions.

4. Identify ways to minimize poor decisions that may lead to long term consequences.

AGENDA

1. Sign-in

2. Snack & Chat

3. Welcome

4. Warm-up

5. Pre-Assessment (optional)

6. Session Introduction
   - ❏ Overview
   - ❏ Objectives
   - ❏ Agenda

7. Lesson
   - ❏ Activity
   - ❏ Recap
   - ❏ Norms
   - ❏ Expectations

8. Close
   - ❏ Post-Assessment
   - ❏ Clean-up
   - ❏ Reflection
   - ❏ Announcements
   - ❏ Parting Pledge

"Manhood is about being present, not perfect." –Phil Black

ACTIVITIES
1. Role Play

ROOM SET-UP	MATERIALS NEEDED
Full or Half Circle Seating	1. Flipchart Paper 2. Dry Erase Board 3. Printing Paper 4. Markers 5. Pens

SESSION PREP

1. Ensure sign-in sheet is ready.

2. Print:
   - ❑ Pre and post assessments
   - ❑ Worksheets/Character Descriptions

3. Set-up transition music.

4. Make sure snacks are ready for distribution.

5. *Write* and post: Objectives, Agenda, Norms & Expectations, and Review Questions on separate sheets of flipchart paper. *If Dry Erase Board is available, use it to write session objectives. Reserve flipchart for the other information.*

"Manhood is about being present, not perfect." –Phil Black

SESSION DETAILS		
1.5 - 2 hr		
	Pre-Session	Set up all materials and music.
3 mins	**Sign-in**	Have students sign in as they enter the designated space.
8 mins	**Snack & Chat**	
3 mins	**Welcome**	Thank students for coming and introduce the warm-up
(optional)	**Highlights and Do-Overs**	
	Review	
8 mins	**Warm-up**	
	Pre Assessment	
2 mins	**Session Introduction**	Today we are going to do a role play activity. We are going to see how administrators and other people in leadership roles, use information to make tough decisions when it comes to student conduct. Our overall objective is to recognize the importance of building a good reputation. In general relationships and as a matter of record or on paper.
30 mins	**Lesson**	In this lesson, students will choose between the following roles: 1. District Superintendent 2. School Principal 3. A Teacher 4. School Board Member 5. Students 1, 2, 3 or 4 *Explain*: Today we are going to reenact a school board review meeting. In this meeting, participants will review the files of four students. Two students are facing disciplinary actions and the remaining students are looking to transfer into the school. After selecting a role, you will review the student's files and give your opinion during the meeting based on what you have read.

"Manhood is about being present, not perfect." –Phil Black

		Note: Both the Superintendent and Principal have special instructions. Do not share them with anyone until after we've completed the entire exercise.
		
		Next: *Distribute* the roles or have students choose who they want to be. Allow time to review the first case file.
		
		Students/characters should be given their own individual meeting with the board. Each character is allowed 2-3 minutes to make a case for why they:
		
		1. Should be given another opportunity to remain in the school/district or
		
		2. Should be given the opportunity to enter into the school/district.
		
		Note: Board members are encouraged to create and ask 2-3 questions to gather additional information for the purpose of making their decision.
		
		Once a satisfactory amount of information has been gathered, the student should be asked to leave while the board deliberates and votes. *Be sure to record all totals.*
		
		Voting options:
		   Students 1 & 2: Detention, suspension, or expulsion.
		   Students 3 & 4: Allow transfer or deny transfer.

5 mins	**Break**	

25 mins	**Close**	Post-Assessment: Have students complete the post assessment. (6 mins)
		
		Clean-up (4 mins)
		
		Reflection: (10 mins)
		
		Example Questions:
		
		  1. While playing the role of an administrator, what information was most important to making your voting decision?
		
		  2. What observations did you make about each student's records?
		
		  3. How has this exercise changed the way you see your personal actions? Past, present, and future?
		
		Announcements (2 mins)
		
		Parting Pledge (2 mins)

"Manhood is about being present, not perfect." –Phil Black

Session 15 Activity Worksheets

(See following pages)

Name: Mr. Stark
Position: Superintendent

Position Description:

The Superintendent is the manager of the School District. They are responsible for making sure the district operates effectively. This includes:

1. Managing finances/money
2. Approving the hiring of teachers, principals, etc.
3. Dealing with major student discipline issues

Personal Information about Mr. Stark

- ❑ Has been married for 10 years
- ❑ Is the father to 3 children
- ❑ Worked as a high school math teacher for eight years before becoming a middle school principal.
- ❑ Successful principal for four years before becoming a superintendent.
- ❑ This is his first year as a superintendent

Character Background

Mr. Stark is the new Superintendent for the Aim High Charter School District. The last Superintendent was fired due to a number of decisions he made while working for the district. The decisions included, but were not limited to: (1) failing to fire the principal of a school that has under- performed for the past three years and (2) showing preferential treatment towards students that were found in violation of district policies.

Activity Instructions

You have been assigned to sit in on a board meeting. The purpose of this meeting is to review the files of four students; two transferring students and two facing disciplinary actions. Your role in this meeting is to observe the principal and decide whether or not if they are a good fit to continue leading the school. You will make this judgement based on their comments and final decisions regarding the students in question.

Note: You may participate within the discussion, but do not make suggestions. If asked for an opinion, simply ask the principal his thoughts, while remaining neutral.

"Manhood is about being present, not perfect." –Phil Black

Name: Mr. Jones
Position: School Principal

Position Description:

The Principal is the manager of a School. They are responsible for making sure the school operates effectively. This includes:

1. Managing finances/money
2. Hiring of teachers, secretaries, maintenance staff, etc.
3. Dealing with student disciplinary issues

Personal Information about Mr. Jones:

- Has been married for 6 years
- Is the father of 4 children
- Worked as a middle school English teacher for 10 years before becoming a principal
- Currently within his third year as principal
- His school's test grades have been the lowest in the district for two years in a row

Character Background

Mr. Jones is the Principal of Rocket High School, of the Aim High school district. Mr. Jones took over two years ago after the previous Principal was re-assigned. Rocket High School has had a number of student disciplinary issues, including petty theft (of cell phones), students bringing weapons or drugs to school, fights, and more. Many feel that Mr. Jones is not tough enough on students, partly because a lot of them are his former middle school students and he knows the families well. He has already been warned that Rocket High School has to show improvement on test scores and do much better when dealing with student conduct.

Activity Instructions

You have been assigned to participate in a board meeting. The purpose of this meeting is to review the files of four students; two transferring students and two facing disciplinary actions. Your roles in this meeting are to:

1. Review the files of each student.

2. Lead a conversation about each, getting feedback from teachers and other present.

3. Make the final decisions on each case.

"Manhood is about being present, not perfect." –Phil Black

Student 1
Name: Melvin Jacobs

Grade: 10th
Cumulative GPA: 1.637
Number of Absences this term: 5 out of 16 days
Total Number of behavior incidents/referrals: 11
Total number of suspensions: 6
Number of days suspended: 27

Incidents:

Date	Incident	Involvement	Reported By	Action
10/4/2014	Theft	Perpetrator	Asst. Principal	5 day suspension
10/25/2014	Disruptive	Perpetrator	Ms. Johnson	ISS
11/13/2014	Fighting	Perpetrator	Asst. Principal	10 day suspension
12/06/2014	Uniform	Perpetrator	Security	1 day suspension
12/12/2014	Skipping	Perpetrator	Principal	ISS
02/10/2015	Language	Perpetrator	Security	Detention
04/21/2015	Disruptive	Perpetrator	Ms. Johnson	Detention
09/27/2015	Gambling	Perpetrator	Mr. Sharper	5 day suspension
10/15/2015	Uniform	Perpetrator	Asst. Principal	2 day suspension
10/23/2015	Skipping	Perpetrator	Principal	Detention
11/16/2015	Drug Poss.	Perpetrator	Security	Board Review

Additional Information:

- ❏ From a single parent household
- ❏ Has five siblings
- ❏ Mother currently unemployed
- ❏ No contact with Father

"Manhood is about being present, not perfect." –Phil Black

Student 2
Name: Jacob Winters

Grade: 11th
Cumulative GPA: 2.837
Number of Absences this term: 1 out of 16 days
Total Number of behavior incidents/referrals: 4
Total number of suspensions: 1
Number of days suspended: 1

Incidents:

Date	Incident	Involvement	Reported By	Action
10/27/2014	Uniform	Perpetrator	Asst. Principal	1 day suspension
03/21/2015	Disruptive	Perpetrator	Mr. Sharper	Detention
11/15/2015	Hall Sweep	Perpetrator	Security	Detention
12/04/2015	Fight	Perpetrator	Principal	Board Review

Most recent incident:

Student was involved in a fight during lunch. Student was not reported as the aggressor, but injured the other party.

Additional information:

- Student is well respected amongst peers and staff
- Very respectful
- Only one suspension since middle school
- Set to participate in a college tour next month
- On track to earn above a 3.0 GPA this card marking

"Manhood is about being present, not perfect." –Phil Black

Student 3 (Transfer)
Name: Dorian Taylor

Grade: 10th
Cumulative GPA: 2.537
Number of Absences this term: 3 out of 16 days
Total Number of behavior incidents/referrals: 6
Total number of suspensions: 2
Number of days suspended: 2

Incidents:

Date	Incident	Involvement	Reported by	Action
09/15/2014	Hall sweep	Perpetrator	Security	Detention
09/27/2014	Uniform	Perpetrator	Asst. Principal	1 day suspension
11/21/2014	Disruptive	Perpetrator	Teacher	Detention
01/10/2015	Hall sweep	Perpetrator	Security	Detention
01/15/2015	Uniform	Perpetrator	Security	1 day suspension
02/04/2015	Drug Poss.	Perpetrator	Security	Expulsion

Most recent incident:

Student was expelled for drug possession.

Additional Information:

- Student Athlete
- Currently on tether/probation for gun possession
- Mostly minor school infractions
- Former school had a strict policy on drugs

"Manhood is about being present, not perfect." –Phil Black

Student 4 (Transfer)
Name: Chauncey Mims

Grade: 11th
Cumulative GPA: 3.43
Number of Absences this term: 0 out of 16 days
Total Number of behavior incidents/referrals: 2
Total number of suspensions: 0
Number of days suspended: 0

Incidents:

Date	Incident	Involvement	Reported by	Action
09/19/2014	Hall sweep	Perpetrator	Security	Detention
11/21/2014	Disruptive	Perpetrator	Teacher	Detention

Most recent incident:

Student talking and making inappropriate comments about teacher.

Additional Information:

- ❏ National Honor Society member
- ❏ Star Athlete
- ❏ Said to be class clown
- ❏ Shows signs of immaturity
- ❏ Performs a lot of community service

"Manhood is about being present, not perfect." –Phil Black

Session 15 Post Assessment

1. Why do people in positions of authority (e.g. a bosses, principals or superintendents) have to make decisions based on facts rather than how they feel?

2. How did this exercise change your view of principals, teachers, etc.?

3. How has this activity changed the way you view your own actions?

"Manhood is about being present, not perfect." –Phil Black

SESSION 16: Assessment, Recognition, and Reflection

Unit 2 S16: Session Objectives

By the end of this session the learner will be able to:

1. Identify the most impactful aspects of Unit II.

2. Share any personal changes made since the first session.

3. Recognize students that have made improvements.

4. Set goals for the next unit.

AGENDA

1. Sign-in

2. Snack & Chat

3. Welcome

4. Q & A

5. Unit Assessment

6. Reactions

7. Recognition

8. Reflection

9. Unit III Overview

10. Close
    - ❏ Clean-up
    - ❏ Announcements
    - ❏ Parting Pledge

"Manhood is about being present, not perfect." –Phil Black

107

ACTIVITIES
1. Unit Assessment 2. Games

ROOM SET-UP	MATERIALS NEEDED
Full or Half Circle Seating	1. Unit Assessment 2. Certificates & Awards (Unit II Completion, Most Improved, and Man of the Month). 3. Dry Erase Board 4. Markers 5. Pens

SESSION PREP
1. Print Unit Assessments. 2. Set-up transition music. 3. Purchase special meal to celebrate.

"Manhood is about being present, not perfect." –Phil Black

SESSION DETAILS		
1.5 - 2 hr		
	Pre-Session	Set up all materials and music.
3 mins	**Sign-in**	Have students sign in as they enter the designated space.
	Snack & Chat	
3 mins	**Welcome**	Thank students for coming and give an overview of the day
(optional)	**Highlights and Do-Overs**	
8 mins	**Q & A**	Answer any questions about the material from past sessions
25 mins	**Unit Assessment**	Administer assessment
6 mins	**Break**	
5 mins	**Reactions**	Any thoughts about the test?
20 mins	**Recognition**	Share words of encouragement- while recognizing each individual and their progress.
3 mins	**Reflection**	What part of Unit II had the biggest impact on you? What personal changes have you made since beginning the program?
8 mins	**Unit III Overview**	
5 mins	**Break**	
8 mins	**Close**	Clean-up (4 mins) Announcements (2 mins) Parting Pledge (2 mins)

"Manhood is about being present, not perfect." –Phil Black

Unit 2 Assessment

1. In the space below, write a reflection on the information that you've learned throughout Unit II regarding Communication. What new terms have you learned? How has your thinking changed? What has impacted you the most from Unit 2?

"Manhood is about being present, not perfect." –Phil Black

Unit 3 The Choice: Education or Prison?

"The greatness of a man is not in how much wealth he acquires, but in his integrity and his ability to affect those around him positively."

-Bob Marley

"Manhood is about being present, not perfect." –Phil Black

Unit 3 Background and Overview

This unit of the curriculum focuses on understanding the **school-to-prison pipeline.** The school-to-prison pipeline describes the increasing patterns of contact students have with juvenile and adult criminal justice systems. These outcomes are usually a result of the practices implemented by schools, such as: zero tolerance policies and the use of police in schools. This phenomenon impacts marginalized communities- especially minority youth. As over-incarceration in the United States has become a serious issue and source of disenfranchisement, addressing the school-to-prison pipeline is extremely important. By exposing students to this practice, this knowledge will assist students in understanding and framing their success within a school environment.

This unit is extremely important mainly because of the direct implications it has for many of our program participants. As behavior in school leads to detrimental consequences, we introduce the prison pipeline to the students as an early intervention and educational tool.

SESSIONS included:

SESSION 17:   Guest Speaker
SESSION 18:   Student One-on-Ones and Self-Care Day
SESSION 19:   Prison Pipeline (History)
SESSION 20:   Buying Habits
SESSION 21:   Prison Pipeline 2 (Today)
SESSION 22:   Prison Pipeline 3 (Pop Culture)
SESSION 23:   Assessing and Selecting Your Circle
SESSION 24:   Unit Assessment, Reflection, and Recognition

"Manhood is about being present, not perfect." –Phil Black

Lesson Plans + Materials

SESSION 17: Guest Speaker

For Guest Speaker Lesson template, see Resource section

"Manhood is about being present, not perfect." –Phil Black

"Manhood is about being present, not perfect." –Phil Black

SESSION 18: Student One-on-Ones

For One-on-One Lesson template, see Resource section

"Manhood is about being present, not perfect." –Phil Black

SESSION 19: Prison Pipeline 1

Unit 3   S19: Session Objectives

By the end of this session the learner will be able to:

1. Discuss the meaning of the phrase: "School to Prison Pipeline."

2. Communicate the importance of slave labor as it relates to the US economy.

3. Express how emancipation impacted business owners and individuals..

AGENDA

1. Sign-in

2. Snack & Chat

3. Welcome

4. Warm-up

5. Pre Assessment (optional)

6. Session Introduction
   - ❑ Overview
   - ❑ Objectives
   - ❑ Agenda

7. Lesson
   - ❑ Activity
   - ❑ Recap
   - ❑ Norms
   - ❑ Expectations

8. Close
   - ❑ Clean-up
   - ❑ Reflection
   - ❑ Announcements
   - ❑ Parting Pledge

"Manhood is about being present, not perfect." –Phil Black

ACTIVITIES

Movie: *Slavery By Another Name*

ROOM SET-UP	MATERIALS NEEDED
Full or Half Circle Seating	1. Flipchart Paper 2. Dry Erase Board 3. Printing Paper 4. Markers 5. Pens 6. AV Equipment 7. *Slavery By Another Name* Documentary 8. SBAN Worksheet

SESSION PREP

1. Ensure sign-in sheet is ready.

2. Print:
   - ❏ Pre and post assessments
   - ❏ Copies of opening and closing pledge

3. Set-up transition music.

4. Make sure snacks are ready to distribute.

5. Write and post Objectives, Agenda and Norms on separate sheets of flipchart paper. *If Dry Erase Board is available, use it to write session objectives. Reserve flipchart for the other information.*

SESSION DETAILS		
1.5 - 2 hr		
	Pre-Session	Set up all materials, music, and AV equipment (with documentary cued).
3 mins	**Sign-in**	Have students sign in as they enter the space.
8 mins	**Snack & Chat**	
3 mins	**Welcome**	Thank students for coming and introduce the warm-up
(optional)	**Highlights and Do-Overs**	
	Review	Optional
15 mins	**Warm-up**	Discussion The objectives of this discussion/exercise is to simplify (and personalize) the multi-dimensional implications of slavery in America as it relates to individuals and their desire to maintain the practice (of slave labor) to maximize earning potential. Introduction *Note: Draw a simple illustration of each point (for visual learners) as you introduce the question.* ❑ Imagine you are a small business owner. ❑ Your company, after paying all bills, earns you and your family $100,000 per year. Questions: 1. How many of you agree that you and your family could have a pretty nice life style with that much money in earnings? 2. Someone share with us a few things that this type of salary would afford you and your family? (*Example answers: Live in a nice home, great neighborhood, drive a nice car, save, etc.*) 3. Imagine you were able to live like this for 10 to 20 years, you would probably get use to it- correct? What if overnight, that $100,000 you were earning was reduced down to $45,000 a year. How would that impact the lifestyle that you have grown to love?

"Manhood is about being present, not perfect." –Phil Black

6 mins	**Pre Assessment**	See attachment
	Introduction	❑ Our next unit is titled: "The Choice: Education or Prison." ❑ You may have been told at one time or another that obtaining an education or going to prison is a choice. Our goal in this section is to actually show you how and why it is a choice; a choice that you decide with every action. ❑ You will hear both commonly used terms, new terms, as well as learning new concepts. ❑ This Unit is ultimately designed to help inform and empower you to make the correct decisions that will place you on the proper path that makes sense for your own life. ❑ This section is little heavier (in terms of information) than the others, so it is imperative that you are more focused than ever. ❑ Are there any questions before we start?
	Break	
5 mins	**Session Introduction**	Question: Who has ever heard of the term "School to Prison Pipeline (SPP)?" *Allow them to make attempts to explain. *Target answer: The SPP is a theory that suggests, there are systems (mainly economic conditions) in place that are designed to direct poor and under-resourced people on a path to prison rather than careers through education.* Today, we are going to take a look at where this theory comes from. We'll begin with a documentary called: "Slavery by Another Name." We won't have time to complete the entire documentary, however, we will pull out the main points for our lesson. As we watch the video, be sure to listen for the answers to the questions on this worksheet. I will stop after the first 10 minutes to discuss your answers.

"Manhood is about being present, not perfect." –Phil Black

| 35 mins | **Lesson** | Questions (1-4): Start – 0:10:05

1. How did the Civil War affect the southern economy?
   A. *The southern economy was devastated.*

2. What was the "primary engine" of the southern economy prior to the Civil War?
   A. *The primary engine of the SE was slave labor.*

3. How much of the region's capital (money) and investments were invested in slavery?
   A. *More than half.*

Pause discussion to ensure all learners have the correct answers.

Question: Think back to our warm up. How do you think slave owners felt, knowing they were about to lose more than half their business?

Continue playing the video

Questions 4 - 7: 0:10:06 – 0:14:12

4. What were the two main worries of former slaveholders?
   A. *People would seek revenge and no one would be around to work.*

5. How did a third of whites view the newly freed slaves?
   A. *As competition.*

6. Why didn't some poor whites like the idea of blacks improving themselves?
   A. *They felt the more blacks gained, the more they would lose.*

7. In what ways would whites now have to compete with blacks? (not explicitly in the video)
   A. *Jobs, businesses, housing, education, etc.* |
|---|---|---|
| 25 mins | **Close** | Post-Assessment: Have students complete the post assessment. (6 mins)

Clean-up (4 mins)

Reflection: (10 mins) |

Primary Take away:

Emancipation created fear and uncertainty for a lot of people. Those who made money by capturing and selling slaves lost money. Business owners, like cotton farmers, would now have to pay someone for their labor. So they too lost money- and almost overnight. Without the free labor, there would be much more competition for good paying jobs.

The question that we will get into during this unit is: How did the economy protect itself from completely collapsing?

Announcements (2 mins)

Parting Pledge (2 mins)

Session 19: Slavery by Another Name Worksheet

1. How did the Civil War affect the southern economy?

2. What was the "primary engine" of the southern economy prior to the Civil War?

3. How much of the region's capital (money) and investments were invested in slavery?

4. What were the two main worries of former slaveholders?

5. How did a third of whites see the newly freed slaves?

6. Why didn't some poor whites like the idea of blacks improving themselves?

7. In what ways would whites now have to compete with blacks?

Session 19 Post Assessment

1. Explain what is meant by the term School to Prison Pipeline.

2. In what ways did slave labor drive the US economy?

3. How were business owner (former slave holders) affected by emancipation?

"Manhood is about being present, not perfect." –Phil Black

SESSION 20: Buying Habits

Unit 3   S20: Session Objectives

By the end of this session the learner will be able to:

1. Share the primary reason businesses exist.

2. Explain the concepts of: Products, services, and a target market.

3. Express the similarities between "buying habits" and general behavior.

4. List the types of "habits" (or behaviors) one would show if he were interested in educational opportunities versus someone interested in crime.

AGENDA

1. Sign-in

2. Snack & Chat

3. Welcome

4. Pre Assessment (optional)

5. Warm-up

6. Session Introduction
   - ❑ Overview
   - ❑ Objectives
   - ❑ Agenda

7. Lesson
   - ❑ Activity
   - ❑ Recap
   - ❑ Norms
   - ❑ Expectations

8. Close
   - ❑ Clean-up
   - ❑ Reflection
   - ❑ Announcements
   - ❑ Parting Pledge

"Manhood is about being present, not perfect." –Phil Black

ACTIVITIES
1. My Favorite 2. Buying Habits

ROOM SET-UP	MATERIALS NEEDED
Full or Half Circle Seating	1. Flipchart Paper 2. Dry Erase Board 3. Printing Paper 4. Markers 5. Pens

SESSION PREP

1. Ensure sign-in sheet is ready.

2. Print:
   - ❏ Pre and post assessments
   - ❏ Buying Habits worksheet
   - ❏ My Favorite worksheet

3. Set-up transition music.

4. Make sure snacks are ready for distribution.

5. *Write* and post: Objectives, Agenda, Norms & Expectations, and Review Questions on separate sheets of flipchart paper. *If Dry Erase Board is available, use it to write session objectives. Reserve flipchart for the other information.*

6. Write out following 3x3 chart on flipchart paper:

Company		
Product/Service		
Target Market		

SESSION DETAILS		
1.5 - 2 hr		
	Pre-Session	Set up all materials and music.
3 mins	**Sign-in**	Have students sign in as they enter the designated space.
8 mins	**Snack & Chat**	
3 mins	**Welcome**	Thank students for coming and introduce the warm-up.
(optional)	**Highlights and Do-Overs**	
	Review	Last session we discussed the impact emancipation had on businesses and individuals. Questions: Why did businesses lose money? *Businesses lost money because more than 50% of the economy was connected to slave labor.* How did it impact individuals? *A third of whites now viewed blacks as competition in the job market.*
	Session Introduction	The goal of this session is to help students see the parallels between being a "consumer" with specific buying habits and an individual who shows a particular pattern of behavior (in school and society). Ultimately, students should walk away with an understanding that: 1. Like traditional companies, both schools and prisons are a business. 2. Similar to the way companies advertise their products to you, after you have shown interest through previous purchases from them in the past (i.e. your buying habits), schools will advertise educational opportunities to those who show interest in learning. 3. In the end, **you** determine your opportunities through the consistency of your behavior, be it good or bad.

"Manhood is about being present, not perfect." –Phil Black

127

8 mins	**Warm-up: My Favorite**	Good job. Today, while we continue to focus on the topic of "The School to Prison Pipeline," we'll deviate for a moment and concentrate on how the SPP is personally affecting us today. Let's get into our warm-up. *pass out worksheets* Have students complete the "My Favorite" worksheet. Note: This worksheet is designed to get students thinking about products they like, or would purchase regularly. *Once students have completed their worksheets, have them share their answers within the group.* Follow-up: Review the list you've made at the top. Is it safe to say that you would buy these products or shop in these places no matter what? Whether they've sent you an advertisement or not? As for the list on the bottom, would you more than likely refrain from purchasing those products or shop in those places? Let's keep this in mind as we continue.
25 mins	**Lesson**	Discussion Why do people go into business for themselves? *Collect answers and record them on flip-chart People go into business for themselves for lots of reasons, but at the end of the day, why does that business exist? *Target: To make money.* How do businesses make money? *Target: By selling products or offering a service.* *Say*: Before we continue, let's recap. You've stated that people go into business for themselves for multiple reasons- the primary reason the business exists is to make money. All businesses make money by selling a "product" or providing a "service." Is that correct? Who do they sell to? *Target: customers.* *Say*: Exactly, but not to just any customer. They advertise to customers that are most likely to buy their product. For example, what type of customer do cereal companies market their products to? *Target: Kids.*

"Manhood is about being present, not perfect." –Phil Black

		Say: Exactly. They do this because they know kids will likely pressure their parents into purchasing that particular cereal. Everyone knows that children love cereal, just as you love the things listed on your worksheet. This is called a target market. Who can tell me what a target market is? *Target: A group of individuals who exhibit the same tendencies or buying habits.* Perfect. Just to be sure we are on the same page, we are going to do another quick exercise. *Pass out the "Buying Habits" worksheet.* *Students are to complete the chart featured on the worksheet.* Once completed. Have volunteers share their answers with the group.
4-6 mins	**Break**	
	Lesson cont'd	Say: You may be asking, what does all of this have to do with the school to prison pipeline? Here it is. *Talking as you fill in the top row of the chart you created. (below) <table><tr><td>Company</td><td>Schools</td><td>Prisons</td></tr><tr><td>Product or service</td><td></td><td></td></tr><tr><td>Target market</td><td></td><td></td></tr></table> Like the traditional businesses you've written about on your worksheets- schools and prisons also make money. Many schools and prisons are privately owned. If we look at schools and prisons like a traditional business: Questions: What would be their products or service? Target: School = Education Prisons = Punishment (for crimes) Who would be their target market? *Target: School = Students who showed interest in learning* *Prison = People who showed criminal behavior.* Conclusion The main points of today are:

		1. Like traditional companies, both schools and prisons are a functioning business; and businesses are designed to make money. For schools, they generate money by providing education to those who want it. Prisons make money by providing punishment to those who commit crimes. 2. Similar to the way companies advertise their products, schools advertise educational opportunities like college access and scholarships to those who show interest in learning. While prisons begin to "recruit" prisoners by observing who displays criminal type behaviors. 3. In the end, *you influence* what opportunities you receive through the consistency of your behaviors.
25 mins	**Close**	Post-Assessment: Have students complete the post assessment (6 mins) Clean-up (4 mins) Reflection (10 mins) Announcements (2 mins) Parting Pledge (2 mins)

"Manhood is about being present, not perfect." –Phil Black

Session 20 Slavery by Another Name Review Assessment

1. How did the Civil War affect the southern economy?

2. The "primary engine" of the southern economy prior to the Civil War?
    a. Cotton

    b. Slave Labor

    c. Police

    d. None of the above

3. What were the two main concerns of former slaveholders?
    a. _____

    b. _____

4. What was the reason that some poor whites like the idea of blacks improving themselves?

Session 20: My Favorites Worksheet
My Favorites

Shoe: _____

Video Game System: _____

Candy Bar: _____

Restaurant: _____

Sports Team: _____

Type of Movie: _____

Phone: _____

Type of Music: _____

My LEAST Favorites (what don't you like)

Shoe: _____

Video Game System: _____

Candy Bar: _____

Restaurant: _____

Sports Team: _____

Type of Movie: _____

Phone: _____

Type of Music: _____

"Manhood is about being present, not perfect." –Phil Black

Session 20 Buying Habits Worksheet

Complete the following chart by filling in the missing information. You may use companies or products you are familiar with.

Business Chart						
Company	Nike (Example)		Apple	Instagram		
Product/Service	Gym Shoes	Barber Shop			Jeans	2K Basketball
Target Market (types of customers)	Athletes					

"Manhood is about being present, not perfect." –Phil Black

Session 20 Post Assessment

1. What is the primary reason a business exists.

2. Businesses make money by selling _____ or providing a
   _____.

3. A target market is a group of people with similar _____.

4. Describe how a person's "buying habits" are similar to other behaviors?

5. What types of habits would a person have if they were interested in learning?

6. What types of habits would a person have if they were going to jail?

"Manhood is about being present, not perfect." –Phil Black

SESSION 21: Prison Pipeline 2 (Today) The Prison Pipeline

Unit 3   S21: Session Objectives

By the end of this session the learner will be able to:

1. Debate the intentions of the 13th amendment (to abolish slavery) and its actual language.

2. Define convict leasing.

3. Recognize the way prisons continue to make profits from prison labor and other means.

4. Express how discussing slavery, prison, and education from an economic perspective will help to make good choices.

AGENDA

1. Sign-in

2. Snack & Chat

3. Welcome

4. Review/Assessment

5. Warm-up

6. Session Introduction
   - Overview
   - Objectives
   - Agenda

7. Lesson
   - Activity
   - Recap
   - Norms
   - Expectations

8. Close
   - Clean-up
   - Reflection
   - Announcements
   - Parting Pledge

"Manhood is about being present, not perfect." –Phil Black

ACTIVITIES

1. Discussion
2. *Slavery By Another Name* (continued)

ROOM SET-UP	MATERIALS NEEDED
Full or Half Circle Seating	1. Flipchart Paper 2. Dry Erase Board 3. Printing Paper 4. Markers 5. Pens 6. Review/Assessment 7. Copies of the Prison Profit Handout 8. AV Equipment 9. *Slavery By Another Name* Documentary 10. SBAN Worksheet

SESSION PREP

1. Ensure sign-in sheet is ready.

2. Print:
   - Review
   - Prison Profit Handout

3. Cue *Slavery by Another Name* video to begin at 0:14:00.

4. Set-up transition music.

5. Make sure snacks are ready for distribution.

6. *Write* and post: Objectives, Agenda, Norms & Expectations, and Review Questions on separate sheets of flipchart paper. *If Dry Erase Board is available, use it to write session objectives. Reserve flipchart for the other information.*

"Manhood is about being present, not perfect." –Phil Black

SESSION DETAILS		
1.5 - 2 hr		
	Pre-Session	Set up all materials and music. *Write* the 13th amendment on the board (or flip-chart): "Neither slavery nor involuntary servitude, except as a punishment for crime whereof the party shall have been duly convicted, shall exist within the United States, or any place subject to their jurisdiction."
3 mins	**Sign-in**	Have students sign in as they enter the designated space.
12 mins	**Snack & Chat**	
3 mins	**Welcome**	Thank students for coming
(optional)	**Highlights and Do-Overs**	
8 mins	**Review**	*See attached assessment*

8 mins	**Warm-up**	*Ask*: By a show of hands, who believes slavery has ended?
		
		  ❑ Take note of who did and did not raise their hands.
		
		  ❑ Divide the room in half by opinion.
		
		  ❑ Instruct students to quietly discuss (within their groups) why they feel as they do.
		
		  ❑ Have both groups write down the main points and to prepare for a group leader to state their case.
		
		  ❑ Once the discussions are over, have students return to their original seats. Then call the group leaders to present their arguments.
		
		Provide relative feedback

6 mins	**Pre Assessment**	

"Manhood is about being present, not perfect." –Phil Black

	Introduction	
	Break	
	Session Introduction	1. Overview: Our first session is simply about gaining an understanding of the program and what is expected. 2. Objectives: Have a volunteer read the objectives, then provide any clarity that you feel is needed. 3. Agenda: After the objectives have been covered, reveal, and recite the agenda.
25 mins	**Lesson**	
25 mins	**Close**	Post-Assessment: Have students complete the post assessment. (6 mins) Clean-up (4 mins) Reflection (10 mins) Announcements (2 mins) Parting Pledge (2 mins)

"Manhood is about being present, not perfect." –Phil Black

Session 21 Post Assessment

1. Explain "convict leasing."

2. What are ways prisons make profits?

3. How has learning about the business side of the prison system (example: earning money by contracting the labor of inmates, while paying them low wages), change your thoughts about advancing in school and finding a career path?

"Manhood is about being present, not perfect." –Phil Black

SESSION 22: Prison Pipeline (Pop Culture)

Unit 3 S22: Objectives

By the end of this session the learner will be able to:

1. Determine the power of imagery.

2. Share how the drug dealer image became a part of the popular culture.

3. List ways to minimize the influence media and technology have on our perception.

AGENDA

1. Sign-in

2. Snack & Chat

3. Session Introduction
   - ❑ Overview
   - ❑ Objectives
   - ❑ Agenda

4. Lesson
   - ❑ Documentary
   - ❑ Discussion

5. Close
   - ❑ Clean-up
   - ❑ Reflection
   - ❑ Announcements
   - ❑ Parting Pledge

ACTIVITIES

1. Documentary: *Planet Rock*
2. Discussion

ROOM SET-UP	MATERIALS NEEDED
Full or Half Circle Seating	1. *Planet Rock*: Documentary: https://youtu.be/zswrGZP7jUY 2. Worksheets 3. Dry Erase Board 4. Markers 5. Pens

"Manhood is about being present, not perfect." –Phil Black

1. Ensure sign-in sheet is ready.

2. Print worksheets.

3. Set-up transition music.

4. Make sure snacks are ready for distribution.

5. *Write* and post: Objectives, Agenda, Norms & Expectations, and Review Questions on separate sheets of flipchart paper. *If Dry Erase Board is available, use it to write session objectives. Reserve flipchart for the other information.*

SESSION DETAILS		
1.5 - 2 hr		
	Pre-Session	Set up all materials and music.
3 mins	**Sign-in**	Have students sign in as they enter the designated space.
15 mins	**Snack & Chat**	
3 mins	**Welcome**	Thank students for coming and introduce the warm-up
(optional)	**Highlights and Do-Overs**	
(optional)	**Review**	
-	**Warm-up:**	
-	**Pre Assessment**	
	Introduction	Today, we'll take a look at the power and influence that drugs and the drug dealer image have on the hip hop culture.
35 mins	**Session**	1. Overview: We are going to watch the documentary titled "*Planet Rock.*" This documentary narrates the story of how the selling of Crack in the 1980's influenced the hip hop culture. 2. Follow along and answer the questions on your worksheet.
15 mins	**Discussion**	In addition to the questions featured on the worksheet, discuss how rap artists, athletes, and others influence our lives?
25 mins	**Close**	Post-Assessment: Have students complete the post assessment. (6 mins) Clean-up (4 mins) Reflection (10 mins) Announcements (2 mins) Parting Pledge (2 mins)

"Manhood is about being present, not perfect." –Phil Black

Session 22 Planet Rock Worksheet

1. How would you describe the conditions of most urban communities (employment, housing, etc.) prior to the crack epidemic?

2. What movie character became the inspiration for many to begin selling drugs?

3. List several movies or songs- that have inspired you to do things in your life?

    _____

    _____

    _____

    _____

4. The movie *Scarface* was described as being "a big commercial to sell crack." What movies or songs do you feel can be described the same way?

5. How did crack affect families?

6. What was meant by the statement: "rappers became like reporters?"

7. What became the new "symbol of status" for rappers and people after the release of *Paid and Full* by Eric B and Rakim?

8. How does trying to live up to the drug dealer image (money, clothes, cars, etc.) affect people in a negative way?

Session 22 Post Assessment

1. How did the drug dealer image become a part of the hip hop culture?

2. How has this information changed the way you view the music and entertainment industry?

"Manhood is about being present, not perfect." –Phil Black

SESSION 23: Assessing and Selecting Your Circle

Unit 3   S23: Session Objectives

By the end of this session the learner will be able to:

1. Identify various types of groups a person can be affiliated with.

2. Explain how others can influence our behaviors.

3. Assess our current circle of friends.

4. Determine the direction (positive or negative) our circles are leading us.

AGENDA

1. Sign-in

2. Snack & Chat

3. Welcome

4. Review

5. Warm-up

6. Pre Assessment

7. Session Introduction
   - Overview
   - Objectives
   - Agenda

8. Lesson
   - Activity

9. Close
   - Post-Assessment
   - Clean-up
   - Reflection
   - Announcements
   - Parting Pledge

"Manhood is about being present, not perfect." –Phil Black

ACTIVITIES
1. Review: (Optional) 2. Warm-Up: What types of groups do people join and why? 3. My Circle Worksheet

ROOM SET-UP	MATERIALS NEEDED
Full or Half Circle Seating	1. Worksheets 2. Flipchart Paper 3. Dry Erase Board 4. Markers 5. Pens

SESSION PREP

1. Ensure sign-in sheet is available.

2. Print: My Circle Worksheets

3. Set-up transition music.

4. Make sure snacks are ready for distribution.

5. *Write* and post Objectives, Agenda, Norms & Expectations, and Review Questions on separate sheets of flipchart paper. *If Dry Erase Board is available, use it to write session objectives. Reserve flipchart for the other information.*

"Manhood is about being present, not perfect." –Phil Black

Session Details		
1.5 - 2 hr		
	Pre-Session	Set up all materials and music.
3 mins	**Sign-in**	Have students sign in as they enter the designated space.
15 mins	**Snack & Chat**	
3 mins	**Welcome**	Thank students for coming
(optional)	**Highlights and Do-Overs**	
	Review	
12 mins	**Warm up**	*Write the following question on flipchart (or a dry erase board):* What types of groups do people join and why? **The purpose of this question is to spark discussion on groups of people we choose to become associated with.*
2 mins	**Introduction**	Today we are going to discuss our circle of influence and how others within that circle can impact our behavior.
20 mins	**Lesson**	There are many groups that we can join within our lifetime, one of those groups would be considered our circle of friends. Just like a club, fraternity or any other group, our friends can influence and shape the type of person we become. Complete the My Circle worksheet. We will discuss your answers after you are finished. **Allow at least 15 minutes. Encourage students to provide detailed answers.*
4 mins	**Break**	
20 mins	**Lesson**	❑ Discuss student answers. ❑ Ask for clarity where needed. Once students have shared their assessments, complete the reflection by:

"Manhood is about being present, not perfect." –Phil Black

		1. Having each person write their answers on the worksheet. Or 2. Ask the questions aloud to the group one by one.
8-10 mins	**Close**	Clean-up (4 mins) Announcements (2 mins) Parting Pledge (2 mins)

"Manhood is about being present, not perfect." –Phil Black

Session 23 My Circle Worksheet

Activity

Consider 1 – 5 friends that you spend the most time with. Using the chart below, describe each friend's attitude towards the four individuals or groups listed (positive or negative). Explain your description by providing an example behavior or regular interaction.

Friend 1

Me	Description	
	Example	
Others	Description	
	Example	
School	Description	
	Example	
Future	Description	
	Example	

Friend 2

Me	Description	
	Example	
Others	Description	
	Example	

"Manhood is about being present, not perfect." –Phil Black

School	Description	
	Example	
Future	Description	
	Example	

Friend 3

Me	Description	
	Example	
Others	Description	
	Example	
School	Description	
	Example	
Future	Description	
	Example	

Friend 4

Me	Description	
	Example	

"Manhood is about being present, not perfect." –Phil Black

Others	Description	
	Example	
School	Description	
	Example	
Future	Description	
	Example	

Friend 5

Me	Description	
	Example	
Others	Description	
	Example	
School	Description	
	Example	
Future	Description	
	Example	

"Manhood is about being present, not perfect." –Phil Black

Reflection

Complete the following statements:

1. After completing this exercise I realize that most of my friends:

2. If someone were to judge me based on the people I hang out with, they would probably think that I:

3. I can make a positive influence with my friends by:

4. I can make sure that I am not being negatively influenced by :

"Manhood is about being present, not perfect." –Phil Black

Session 23 Post Assessment

1. What groups would (or are you) participating in that support the direction you want to take in life?

2. Explain the importance of your "circle?"

SESSION 24: Assessment, Recognition, and Reflection

Unit 3   S24: Session Objectives

By the end of this session the learner will be able to:

1. Identify the aspects of Unit III that made the most impact on you.

2. Share any changes that you've made since the first session.

3. Recognize students that have made improvements.

4. Set goals for the next unit.

AGENDA

1. Sign-in

2. Welcome

3. Q & A

4. Unit Assessment

5. Reactions

6. Recognition

7. Reflection

8. Unit VI Overview

9. Close
    - ❏ Clean-up
    - ❏ Announcements
    - ❏ Parting Pledge

"Manhood is about being present, not perfect." –Phil Black

ACTIVITIES
1. Unit Assessment 2. Games

ROOM SET-UP	MATERIALS NEEDED
Full or Half Circle Seating	1. Unit Assessment 2. Certificates & Awards (Unit V Completion, Most Improved, and Man of the Month). 3. Dry Erase Board 4. Markers 5. Pens

SESSION PREP
1. Print Unit Assessments. 2. Set-up transition music. 3. Get special meal to celebrate.

"Manhood is about being present, not perfect." –Phil Black

		SESSION DETAILS	
1.5 - 2 hr			
	Pre-Session	Set up all materials and music.	
3 mins	**Sign-in**	Have students sign in as they enter the designated space.	
3 mins	**Welcome**	Thank students for coming and give an overview of the day	
(optional)	**Highlights and Do-Overs**		
8 mins	**Q & A**	Answer any questions about the material from the past sessions	
25 mins	**Unit Assessment**	Administer assessment	
6 mins	**Break**		
5 mins	**Reactions**	*Ask*: Any thoughts about the test?	
20 mins	**Recognition**	Share words of encouragement while recognizing each individual and their progress.	
3 mins	**Reflection**	What part of Unit III was most significant for you? What personal changes have you made since starting?	
8 mins	**Unit IV Overview**		
5 mins	**Break**		
8 mins	**Close**	Clean-up (4 mins) Announcements (2 mins) Parting Pledge (2 mins)	

"Manhood is about being present, not perfect." –Phil Black

Unit 3 Assessment

Below, write a personal reflection on the information you've learned from Unit III- on the School to Prison Pipeline. What new terms have you learned? How has your thinking changed? What information left the biggest impact on you?

"Manhood is about being present, not perfect." –Phil Black

Unit 4: The Importance of Showing Up (Presence Over Perfection)

"Community cannot for long feed on itself; it can only flourish with the coming of others from beyond, their unknown and undiscovered brothers."

-Howard Thurman

"Manhood is about being present, not perfect." –Phil Black

Unit 4 Background and Overview

This unit focuses on the behaviors and mindsets that reflect the TMP model of being present and not perfect. In this unit, students will learn how to maintain engagement in everyday environments, even when challenges present themselves. Students will also learn how to fully participate as a functional member within their communities (family, school, teams), and embrace the impact of giving through community service.

These lessons and activities are important, mainly because challenges often deter people from continuing involvement in positive activities and engagement with others within their communities. By reinforcing strategies and the mindset of not striving for perfection, we can arm the students with behaviors to remain present in their environments.

Here's a list of the sessions included within this unit:

SESSION 25:   Guest Speaker
SESSION 26:   Student 1:1's and Self-Care Day
SESSION 27-28:   Be Present
SESSION 29:   My Support
SESSION 30:   Outreach Activity/Community Engagement
SESSION 31:   Service Debrief
SESSION 32:   Unit Review, Reflection, and Recognition

"Manhood is about being present, not perfect." –Phil Black

Lesson Plans + Materials

"Manhood is about being present, not perfect." –Phil Black

SESSION 25: Guest Speaker

For Guest Speaker Lesson template, visit the Resource section

"Manhood is about being present, not perfect." –Phil Black

SESSION 26: Student One -on-Ones

For One-on-One Lesson templates, please visit the Resource section

"Manhood is about being present, not perfect." –Phil Black

SESSION 27 - 28: Be Present

Unit 4   S27 - 28: Session Objectives

By the end of these sessions the learner will be able to:

1. List the positive qualities modeled by the character Christopher Gardner.

2. Express how the character Christopher Gardner lived the motto and virtues of The Manhood Project.

3. Explain how to begin taking on those same qualities.

4. Identify people who display the positive qualities listed.

AGENDA

1. Sign-in

2. Snack & Chat

3. Welcome

4. Warm-up

5. Pre Assessment (optional)

6. Session Introduction
   - Overview
   - Objectives

7. Lesson
   - Movie
   - Discussion

8. Close
   - Clean-up
   - Reflection
   - Announcements
   - Parting Pledge

"Manhood is about being present, not perfect." –Phil Black

ACTIVITIES

1. Movie: *The Pursuit of Happiness*
2. Reflective Exercise: Connect the motto and virtues of TMP to Chris

ROOM SET-UP	MATERIALS NEEDED
Full or Half Circle Seating	1. Movie 2. Notebook paper/Journals 3. Pens

SESSION PREP

1. Ensure sign-in sheet is ready.

2. Print:
   - ❏ Pre and post assessments

3. Set-up transition music.

4. Make sure snacks are ready to distribute.

5. Set-up audio visual equipment and cue movie.

6. Make sure students have their manuals ready.

7. Cut six small strips of paper. Write the motto on one, then one of the five virtues on the others.

SESSION DETAILS		
3 - 4 hr		
	Pre-Session	Set up all materials and music.
3 mins	**Sign-in**	Have students sign in as they enter the designated space.
15 mins	**Snack & Chat**	
3 mins	**Welcome**	Thank students for coming and introduce the warm-up
(optional)	**Highlights and Do-Overs**	
6 mins	**Pre Assessment**	
	Session Introduction	Overview: To kick off our unit on being "present versus being perfect," we are going to watch a movie and have a discussion throughout.
25 mins	**Lesson**	Define Responsibility To begin, who can tell us what "responsibility" is? *Target answer: *Responsibility is something a task or role that a person has to fulfill (or something similar).* Once defined, have students provide examples to check understanding: What is a responsibility that a _____ (teacher, parent, police officer, etc.) would have? *Target: *To educate students, to provide for their kids, to protect the community, etc.* Now have them list examples relative to the topic: Who can give examples of responsibilities that a man would or should have? *Target: *The Five Virtues.* After the brief discussion, *say*: This unit is designed to help us really understand this concept of: being

"Manhood is about being present, not perfect." –Phil Black

165

		present. Instruct students to: 1. Turn to page _____ of their journals. 2. Explain the answers to the questions on the page, as they appear in order throughout the movie. 3. We will stop the movie at different points to take breaks and discuss some of your answers throughout. Play movie ❏ Stopping point 1: After Chris's car gets towed, discuss the first two questions listed on the worksheet. ❏ Stopping point 2: Chris tells his son: "If you want something, go get it."
	Break	
		(After stopping point 2): Discuss questions 3-5. ❏ Stopping point 3: Chris cries in the bathroom holding Christopher. Discuss questions 6 & 7. *Explain*: We will not have any more stops. We will save the rest of the discussion for the end. Final Discussion: 1. Have students break into equal groups of six. 2. Hand each group a slip of paper that contains the program motto or one of the five virtues. 3. Instruct students to discuss how Chris experienced or portrayed what is listed on their paper. 4. Have each group share their answers.
	Break	

"Manhood is about being present, not perfect." –Phil Black

| 25 mins | **Close (for both sessions)** | Post-Assessment: Have students complete the post assessment. (6 mins)

Clean-up (4 mins)

Reflection: How has the Christopher Gardner story affected the way you currently see yourself and the way you want to see yourself in the future? (10 mins)

Announcements (2 mins)

Parting Pledge (2 mins) |
|---|---|---|

"Manhood is about being present, not perfect." –Phil Black

Session 27 and 28 Pursuit of Happiness Discussion Questions

1. What did Chris make up in his mind as a kid?

2. How would you feel if you were Chris at the point in the story where his car got towed away?

3. What are possible reasons for Linda treating Chris with disrespect?

4. Why do you think Chris was so determined to have his son?

5. While on the playground, what did Chris tell Christopher never to do?

6. What was going through Chris's mind in the bathroom?

7. How would you describe Christopher Gardner as a man at this point in the movie?

"Manhood is about being present, not perfect." –Phil Black

SESSION 29: My Support

Unit 4   S29: Session Objectives

By the end of this session the learner will be able to:

1. Identify the individuals that have aided in your personal growth and development.

2. Discuss the impact others have made in our lives.

3. Share the benefits of helping others in need.

4. Determine what it means to be "an active citizen" in our society.

AGENDA

1. Sign-in

2. Snack & Chat

3. Welcome

4. Pre Assessment (optional)

5. Warm-up

6. Session Introduction
   - Overview
   - Objectives
   - Agenda

7. Lesson
   - Activity
   - Recap
   - Norms
   - Expectations

8. Close
   - Clean-up
   - Reflection
   - Announcements
   - Parting Pledge

"Manhood is about being present, not perfect." –Phil Black

ACTIVITIES

1. Pair Share
2. My Support Worksheet

ROOM SET-UP	MATERIALS NEEDED
Full or Half Circle Seating	1. Index Cards 2. My Support Worksheet 3. Loose-leaf paper 4. Flipchart (or dry erase board) 5. Markers 6. Pens

SESSION PREP

1. Ensure sign-in sheet is ready.

2. Print:
   - ❏ Pre and post assessments
   - ❏ Copies of opening and closing pledge

3. Set-up transition music.

4. Make sure snacks are ready for distribution.

5. *Write* and post: Objectives, Agenda, Norms & Expectations, and Review Questions on separate sheets of flipchart paper. *If Dry Erase Board is available, use it to write session objectives. Reserve flipchart for the other information.*

6. Designate one index card per participant.

7. Print out the "My Support" Worksheets.

Additional Prep

8. Prior to the session, set up a service project or volunteer opportunity for the group. This project should be one that will give space for learning (through participation)- the needs and benefits to helping others.

9. Print permission slips for each student.

"Manhood is about being present, not perfect." –Phil Black

SESSION DETAILS		
1.5 - 2 hr		
	Pre-Session	Set up all materials and music.
3 mins	**Sign-in**	Have students sign in as they enter the designated space.
15 mins	**Snack & Chat**	
3 mins	**Welcome**	Thank students for coming and introduce the warm-up
(optional)	**Highlights and Do-Overs**	
	Review	
8 mins	**Warm-up: My Hero**	My Hero ❑ Give each student an index card and pen. ❑ Instruct them to do the following: 1. Think of someone you admire or look-up to. This can be anyone- a parent, guardian, family member, friend, or famous person. 2. Without writing their name, explain why you admire them. List as many reasons or personal qualities that you can think of. *Provide 4 – 6 minutes (or additional time if needed) for this part of the activity.* 3. Once students have recorded their answers, have them select a partner to do a "pair-share" of their answers. *3 – 5 minutes for this portion.* 4. Now, ask for at-least 4 volunteers to share with the group.
6 mins	**Pre Assessment**	

"Manhood is about being present, not perfect." –Phil Black

	Break	
	Session Introduction	Today we are going to discuss the importance supporting others and giving back. We will do this by leaning on our own experiences through identifying key individuals who have and continue to help us in our growth and development.
25 mins	**Lesson**	❑ Pass out the "My Support" worksheets. ❑ Instruct the learners to: 1. Read the directions and complete the worksheet. 2. Answer each question fully. Provide an extra piece of loose-leaf paper (if additional writing space is needed). 3. Allow 12 - 15 minutes for uninterrupted writing. Report out (10 - 12 mins) 1. Encourage each student to share at least 1 response. 2. Remind students that the group norm **NOSTUESO** is in effect. 3. After each student has shared one answer, if time allows, have those interested in doing so- to share more.
25 mins	**Close**	Post-Assessment: Have students complete the post assessment (6 mins) Clean-up (4 mins) Reflection (2-3 mins) Question: What do the people listed on your paper get in return for helping and supporting you? *If clarity is needed ask: "Or what are the benefits to helping and supporting others in need?" *Sample Answer:* *Satisfaction in seeing their needs met.* Closing Comment: The main point of today: The people that have helped and supported your personal growth- not only recognized the need, but made the decision to take action. Like your selves, there are many others that need support, unfortunately in many cases- they don't have anyone willing to assist them, in obtaining the foundation that they need. This is why we're going

"Manhood is about being present, not perfect." –Phil Black

to practice what we've learned by participating in a volunteer/service activity.

Being a participant assists you in being viewed as a productive, valued, and active citizen of society.

Give an overview of the service project that you have selected. Hand out permission slips (if applicable).

Announcements (2 mins)

Parting Pledge (2 mins)

Session 29 My Support Worksheet

Using the chart below, list 3 to 5 individuals who regularly support your growth and development as a young man. Then answer the three questions that follow. An example is provided below.

Name or title (Optional)	In what ways does this person help or support you?	How has their support helped you to grow and develop?	How would your life be different without their support?
Example Uncle	❑ Teaches me about life ❑ Takes me to ball games	The lessons my uncle taught, helps me to know right from wrong. When I get to spend time with him, I learn how a man is supposed to behave, and it helps me feel loved.	I wouldn't have a man close to me, in my life to show me things. I would probably make more mistakes.

"Manhood is about being present, not perfect." –Phil Black

Session 29 Post Assessment

1. How does recognizing those who support you, affect your attitude, thoughts, and behaviors towards others?

2. After recognizing the support that you receive, how much more likely are you to help others? Explain.

3. What does it mean to be an active and productive citizen of society?

"Manhood is about being present, not perfect." –Phil Black

SESSION 30: Outreach Activity/Community Engagement

Unit 4   S30: Supporting Others

Session 30 is reserved for a group volunteer experience. As the facilitator, you must coordinate a project that will allow the learners to get the experience of supporting others (in need). This lesson plan will serve as a guide to assist you in the planning of the project.

Note: Partnering with a local agency (e.g. food banks, soup kitchens) is an excellent way to ensure students will gain the desired learning experience, while minimizing time, and efforts to prepare.

PROJECT TITLE

Projects may include (but are not limited to):

- ❑   A Near-Peer mentoring session (of a younger student)
- ❑   Homework help
- ❑   Campus/Community Beautification
- ❑   Feed the homeless and less fortunate

Project Title: _____

OVERVIEW

Briefly describe what the students will be doing.

LOCATION	LOGISTICS	
	DATE: DURATION: PHONE:	START TIME: CONTACT: EMAIL:

"Manhood is about being present, not perfect." –Phil Black

PRE PROJECT

1. Solidify all details.

2. Create a permission slip or letter to parents.

3. Follow up with the point of contact at least once to confirm, prior to the project date.

4. Ensure transportation is set (if applicable).

5. Make sure supplies are in a secured space (if applicable).

DURING PROJECT

1. Start with a huddle to:

❏ Review group norms and expectations

❏ Communicate the specific lessons you aim for them to draw out of the experience.

❏ To give any specific project assignments or details.

2. Monitor students to ensure they remain on task and engaged.

POST PROJECT

1. Have students clean before leaving.

2. Prepare them to talk about the experience in the next session.

3. Thank the partnering agency.

"Manhood is about being present, not perfect." –Phil Black

SESSION 31: Service Debrief

Unit 5   S31: Session Objectives

By the end of this session the learner will be able to:

1. Share the aspects of service enjoyed most.

2. Discuss what lessons were learned by helping others.

3. Express ways to improve the experience.

AGENDA

1. Sign-in

2. Snack & Chat

3. Welcome

4. Pre Assessment (optional)

5. Warm-up

6. Session Introduction
   - ❏ Overview
   - ❏ Objectives
   - ❏ Agenda

7. Lesson
   - ❏ Activity
   - ❏ Recap
   - ❏ Norms
   - ❏ Expectations

8. Close
   - ❏ Clean-up
   - ❏ Reflection
   - ❏ Announcements
   - ❏ Parting Pledge

"Manhood is about being present, not perfect." –Phil Black

ACTIVITIES
1. Warm-up: Share or Ask 2. Like, Love, Learn, and Change

ROOM SET-UP	MATERIALS NEEDED
Full or Half Circle Seating	1. Flipchart Paper 2. Dry Erase Board 3. 3L's & Change Worksheet 4. Post-it paper 5. (1) Small zip-lock bag 6. Markers 7. Pens

SESSION PREP

1. Ensure sign-in sheet is available.

2. Print:
   - ❏ Pre and post assessments
   - ❏ Copies of opening and closing pledge

3. Set-up transition music.

4. Make sure snacks are ready for distribution.

5. Write and post: Objectives, Agenda, Norms & Expectations, and Review Questions on separate sheets of flipchart paper. *If Dry Erase Board is available, use it to write session objectives. Reserve flipchart for the other information.*

6. Write the following questions/Statements on individual post-it notes.
   - ❏ The last time I helped someone in need was...
   - ❏ Someone helped me most recently by…
   - ❏ I remember needing help with _____ but couldn't get it. I felt...
   - ❏ When a person refuses my help it make me feel…
   - ❏ Fold each paper twice to hide the questions.
   - ❏ Place them in the Zip-lock bag

"Manhood is about being present, not perfect." –Phil Black

SESSION DETAILS			
1.5 - 2 hr			
	Pre-Session	Set up all materials and music.	
3 mins	**Sign-in**	Have students sign in as they enter the designated space.	
15 mins	**Snack & Chat**		
3 mins	**Welcome**	Thank students for coming and introduce the warm-up	
(optional)	**Highlights and Do-Overs**		
	Review		
10-20 mins	**Warm-up: Share or Ask**	*Explain:* We are about to play: Share or Ask. In this bag I have four questions. We are going to start by: 1. Passing the bag around to one person at a time. 2. When you have the bag, pull a statement without looking. 3. Read the statement out loud. 4. You then have the option of completing the statement yourself or posing it as a question to someone else within the group. Example: I pull the statement: "The last time I helped someone in need…" I can complete the statement by sharing: "I helped Ms. Carter carry her bags this morning." Or I can ask John: "When was the last time you helped someone in need?" *Suggest 1-2 rounds (depending on the length of discussion).*	
6 mins	**Pre Assessment**		
	Break		

"Manhood is about being present, not perfect." –Phil Black

	Session Introduction	Last week we had the opportunity to participate in a service project. Today we are going to talk about your experience.
25 mins	**Lesson**	1. We are going to take a few minutes to write down four areas of reflection. 2. On this worksheet I want you to write what you: Liked, Loved, Learned and would change about the service we did. -12 to 15 minutes Once everyone has finished, have students share their responses. Be sure to ask follow-up questions to challenge their thinking when appropriate, while making relevant, and encouraging statements as needed.
25 mins	**Close**	Post-Assessment: Have students complete the post assessment (6 mins) Clean-up (4 mins) Reflection (10 mins) *Conclusion: Helping others is need. Not only for the those who are receiving the help, but also for those who give. Acts of kindness and supporting others adds to our character and shapes who we are as humans. Announcements (2 mins) Parting Pledge (2 mins)

"Manhood is about being present, not perfect." –Phil Black

Service Debrief Worksheet

Using the prompts below, write a reflection of your service experience:

1. I liked

2. I loved

3. I learned

4. I would change

Additional Feedback:

"Manhood is about being present, not perfect." –Phil Black

SESSION 32: Assessment, Recognition, and Reflection

Unit 4   S32: Session Objectives

By the end of this session the learner will be able to:

1. Identify the most impactful aspects of Unit IV.

2. Share any personal changes made since the first session.

3. Recognize students that have made improvements.

4. Set goals for the next unit.

AGENDA

1. Sign-in

2. Welcome

3. Q & A

4. Unit Assessment

5. Reactions

6. Recognition

7. Reflection

8. Unit V Overview

9. Close
   - ❏ Clean-up
   - ❏ Announcements
   - ❏ Parting Pledge

"Manhood is about being present, not perfect." –Phil Black

ACTIVITIES
1. Unit Assessment 2. Games

ROOM SET-UP	MATERIALS NEEDED
Full or Half Circle Seating	1. Unit Assessment 2. Certificates & Awards (Unit IV Completion, Most Improved, and Man of the Month). 3. Dry Erase Board 4. Markers 5. Pens

SESSION PREP
1. Print Unit Assessments. 2. Set-up transition music. 3. Get special meal to celebrate.

"Manhood is about being present, not perfect." –Phil Black

SESSION DETAILS		
1.5 - 2 hr		
	Pre-Session	Set up all materials and music.
3 mins	**Sign-in**	Have students sign in as they enter the space.
3 mins	**Welcome**	Thank students for coming and give an overview of the day
(optional)	**Highlights and Do-Overs**	
8 mins	**Q&A**	Answer any questions about the material from the past sessions
25 mins	**Unit Assessment**	Administer assessment
6 mins	**Break**	
5 mins	**Reactions**	Any thoughts about the test?
20 mins	**Recognition**	Share words of encouragement while recognizing each individual and their progress.
3 mins	**Reflection**	What part of Unit IV was most impactful for you?
		What personal changes have you made since we started?
8 mins	**Unit V Overview**	
5 mins	**Break**	
8 mins	**Close**	Clean-up (4 mins)
		Announcements (2 mins)
		Parting Pledge (2 mins)

"Manhood is about being present, not perfect." –Phil Black

Unit 5: Living the Five Virtues

"I prefer to be true to myself, even at the hazard of incurring the ridicule of others, rather than to be false, and to incur my own abhorrence."

-Frederick Douglass

"Manhood is about being present, not perfect." –Phil Black

Unit 5 Background and Overview

The Manhood Project is built upon the **Five Virtues** of manhood that reflect behavior showing high moral standards. Theses virtues -- love, respect, courage, provision, and protection -- combine into a foundation of standards that will guide intentions and motivations.

At this point in the curriculum, the lessons will address not only specific behavior and awareness, but setting everyday principles of intention. These intentions require an emotional intelligence (acquired from previous lessons within the guide) that will continue to increase and guide the students well into their future.

SESSION'S included within this unit:

SESSION 33:   Guest Speaker
SESSION 34:   Student 1:1s and Self-Care Day
SESSION 35:   Establishing a Moral Code
SESSION 36:   Love
SESSION 37:   Respect (Part I)
SESSION 38:   Respect (Part II)
SESSION 39:   Respect (Part III)
SESSION 40:   Courage, Provision, and Protection
SESSION 41:   Unit Assessment, Reflection, and Recognition

"Manhood is about being present, not perfect." –Phil Black

Lesson Plans + Materials

"Manhood is about being present, not perfect." –Phil Black

SESSION 33: Guest Speaker

For the Guest Speaker Lesson template, please visit the Resource section

"Manhood is about being present, not perfect." –Phil Black

SESSION 34: Student One-on-Ones

For the One-on-One Lesson template, please see the Resource section

"Manhood is about being present, not perfect." –Phil Black

SESSION 35: Establishing a Moral Code

Unit 5   S35: Session Objectives

By the end of this session the learner will be able to:

1. Define Moral Code.

2. Determine how we are currently being guided in our lives outside of the program.

3. Recognize the importance of being properly guided by others (through mentorship), and ourselves (internally through our moral code).

4. Identify the 5 Virtues as a framework for establishing a personal moral code.

AGENDA

1. Sign-in

2. Snack & Chat

3. Welcome

4. Pre Assessment (optional)

5. Warm-up

6. Session Introduction
   - ❏ Overview
   - ❏ Objectives
   - ❏ Agenda

7. Lesson
   - ❏ Activity
   - ❏ Recap
   - ❏ Norms
   - ❏ Expectations

8. Close
   - ❏ Clean-up
   - ❏ Reflection
   - ❏ Announcements
   - ❏ Parting Pledge

"Manhood is about being present, not perfect." –Phil Black

ACTIVITIES

1. Warm-up: Arrow and The Archer (Puzzle & Discussion)
2. How am I Guided?

ROOM SET-UP	MATERIALS NEEDED
❑ Start: Tables/Desks for groups of 4-6 (for warm up activity) ❑ Full or Half Circle Seating for discussion	1. Copies of the Archer Image 2. (4) Sheets of printing paper 3. Flip Chart or Dry Erase Board 4. Markers 5. Pens 6. Tape

SESSION PREP

1. Ensure sign-in sheet is available.

2. Set-up transition music.

3. Make sure snacks are ready for distribution.

4. *Write* and post: Objectives, Agenda, Norms & Expectations and Review Questions on separate sheets of flipchart paper. *If Dry Erase Board is available, use it to write session objectives.*

5. Print copies of the Archer Image.
   - ❑ 1 Copy for the facilitator.
   - ❑ 1 Copy for each predetermined small group (for the activity)

6. Cut the copies of the Archer image designated for the groups into 4 equal (puzzle) pieces.

7. Using the four sheets of printing paper, separately write (by hand or type in large letters):
   - ❑ Properly-guided
   - ❑ Misguided
   - ❑ Self-guided
   - ❑ Unguided

8. Post the "guided" terms on the wall in four separate areas of the room.
   These will be used as signs later to direct students during the main activity.

9. *Write and post the following definitions on (2) separate flip-chart sheets.*
   - ❑ Moral Code (on one sheet): is a set of rules or a code of conduct which governs how an individual should act within a community or group.[2]

   (The following on the second sheet.)

---

[2] http://psychologydictionary.org/

"Manhood is about being present, not perfect." –Phil Black

- ❑ Properly-guided: Someone who has positive support leading them in the right direction.

- ❑ Misguided: A feeling of being led in a negative or harmful direction.

- ❑ Self-guided: One who feels forced to make most or all decisions on their own, due to a lack of support and guidance.

- ❑ Unguided: The feeling of being lost, and having no direction.

SESSION DETAILS

1.5 - 2 hr		
	Pre-Session	Set up all materials and music.
3 mins	**Sign-in**	Have students sign in as they enter the designated space.
8 mins	**Snack & Chat**	
3 mins	**Welcome**	Thank students for coming and introduce the warm-up
(optional)	**Highlights and Do-Overs**	
	Review	
8 mins	**Warm-up:**	The objective of this activity is to help the learner recognize the need for mentorship and overall guidance. 1. Separate the groups into teams of 4 to 6 (based on the number of participants). 2. Give each group a set of puzzle pieces (that form the Archer image) and tape. 3. Be sure to scramble them before distributing. 4. Instruct the students to collectively put the puzzle together. 5. The group to successfully create (a taped) Archer image the fastest wins. Follow up questions/discussion *This set of questions are about setting goals. 1. What do you see in this picture? This question is simply to get the learner thinking. Be prepared Initially for very general and surface answers. Encourage them to look deeper? Possible follow up questions may include: 1. Where is he aiming? 2. Is he looking to hit a target, or just aiming in the sky?

"Manhood is about being present, not perfect." –Phil Black

		3. If the sky, what would be the point?
		4. Have you ever felt like you were just doing something for the sake of doing it?
		Learning point: In order to be successful at anything, you must have a goal. By participating in this program, one of your goals is to become the best version of yourself possible.
		*Transition: However, what if you have a goal to do something, with no idea of how to do it?
		Questions: This set of questions sets up the point of needing help, to achieve our goals.
		1. Has anyone ever shot a bow and arrow?
		2. What if you had a target to hit with the arrow, but you've never shot an arrow before?
		3. How would you hit your target?
		Possibilities: Self- taught, watching someone else who may be doing the same thing, or (target answer): Ask someone else who has done it before.
		Point: Often times we feel alone and that we have to do things by ourselves. The best way for us to learn (even about ourselves), is by seeking guidance from someone older and wiser. We use their teachings to empower us to make decisions on our own.
6 mins	**Pre Assessment**	
	Introduction	In this unit we are going to go deeper into what it means to live the 5 Virtues. Part of that process is understanding what the 5 Virtues represent and how to use them as a guide to create and shape your own personal value system. Today we are going to start by uncovering what it means to have a moral code.
	Break	
	Session Introduction	In our warm-up we:
		1. Identified the need to have a goal, and

"Manhood is about being present, not perfect." –Phil Black

		2. Discussed the best way to achieve our goals is to learn from other's that may have already achieved the goals that we have set. In this next exercise we are going to identify the type of guidance we are currently receiving outside of this program. So far, we have imagined ourselves being the one shooting the arrow. For this part, image that you (yourselves) are the arrow, and the person aiming you in a direction is the person who has influence in your life. It could be a parent, teacher, or even a peer. Just for a moment, think about "who" is guiding you outside of this space. *Allow a brief moment to process.*
25 mins	**Lesson**	Now, we are going to do a little activity. Around the room we have 4 sheets of paper. *Reveal each sign (if they are not already visible) and simply read them. ❑ Properly Guided ❑ Misguided ❑ Self-guided ❑ Unguided *Also reveal the flip chart, which holds the definition for each and have someone read them out loud. Instructions: I want you to go to the area that best describes how you feel most often. 1. If you feel your parents or the people influencing you are there for you and pointing you in the right direction, go to "Properly Guided." 2. If you feel the people in your life have been sending you in the wrong direction, go to "Misguided." 3. If you feel as if you can only count on yourself, and you are making your own decisions most of the time, go to "Self-Guided." 4. If you feel that you don't have anyone and you are just kind of wandering along, go to "Unguided." Once students have gone to their spaces, have them talk amongst themselves about why they chose that space.

"Manhood is about being present, not perfect." –Phil Black

		In cases where only one student chooses a space, go and discuss their choice with him (or have him join another group, still using the topic he chose). Allow 4-6 minutes for discussion. *Bring everyone back to the circle. Now ask students to share their answers. *Give relevant feedback to each one, while looking to connect their answers to the need to identify proper guidance from positive influences.* Once everyone has finished sharing their answers, thank them for participating, and provide a short break (if needed) before giving closing remarks.
25 mins	**Close**	Post-Assessment: Have students complete the post assessment (6 mins) Clean-up (4 mins) Reflection: (10 mins) * *Reveal the flip-chart with the definition for Moral Code and have someone to read it.* Closing Point: The best way for us to achieve our goals, is by making sure we have the right people in our lives to give us proper guidance. Through their teachings we are better equipped to establish our own moral code. That is exactly what the 5 Virtues represent: a benchmark or example set of standards- to use as within our lives. Next session, we will begin to talk about how to do that. Announcements: (2 mins) Instruct the group to create (or bring) something (e.g. a drawing, song, poem) that represents them or how they view themselves. Parting Pledge (2 mins)

"Manhood is about being present, not perfect." –Phil Black

"Manhood is about being present, not perfect." –Phil Black

Session 35 Post Assessment

1. What does it mean to have a moral code?

2. Why is it important to be aware of the "guidance" you are receiving?

3. What qualities (of a person who is looking to influence you) should you pay attention to?

"Manhood is about being present, not perfect." –Phil Black

SESSION 36: Love

Unit 5   S36: Session Objectives

By the end of this session the learner will be able to:

1. Define: Love for self, family, others, and community.

2. Communicate the importance of loving one's self- first.

3. Identify ways to demonstrate love.

4. Recognize how to love others, without losing love for self.

AGENDA

1. Sign-in

2. Snack & Chat

3. Welcome

4. Pre Assessment (optional)

5. Warm-up

6. Session Introduction
    - Overview
    - Objectives
    - Agenda

7. Lesson
    - Activity
    - Recap
    - Norms
    - Expectations

8. Close
    - Clean-up
    - Reflection
    - Announcements
    - Parting Pledge

"Manhood is about being present, not perfect." –Phil Black

ACTIVITIES
1. Warm-up: If I were a…   2. What is Love worksheet

ROOM SET-UP	MATERIALS NEEDED
Full or Half Circle Seating	1. Flipchart Paper 2. Dry Erase Board 3. Printing Paper 4. Markers 5. Pens

SESSION PREP

1. Ensure sign-in sheet is available.

2. Print:
   - ❑ Pre and post assessments
   - ❑ Copies of opening and closing pledge

3. Set-up transition music.

4. Make sure snacks are ready for distribution.

5. *Write* and post: Objectives, Agenda, Norms & Expectations, and Review Questions on separate sheets of flipchart paper. *If Dry Erase Board is available, use it to write session objectives. Reserve flipchart for the other information.*

"Manhood is about being present, not perfect." –Phil Black

SESSION DETAILS		
1.5 - 2 hr		
	Pre-Session	Set up all materials and music.
3 mins	**Sign-in**	Have students sign in as they enter the designated space.
15 mins	**Snack & Chat**	
3 mins	**Welcome**	Thank students for coming and introduce the warm-up
(optional)	**Highlights and Do-Overs**	
	Review	
15-20 mins	**Warm-up: If I were A...**	Last week, we asked that you create or bring a form of art or an object that represents you or how you feel about yourself. Now, we'll share objects. 1. Ask for a volunteer to start. 2. Before beginning, instruct the student to use the phrase "If I were a (**state the type of object they chose**), I would be (**state the specific object chosen**). ❏ Example: *If I were a **song**, I would be **"Comin' From Where I'm From" by Anthony Hamilton**.* 3. Continue until all prepared and willing participants have shared.
6 mins	**Pre Assessment**	
	Introduction	
	Break	
	Session Introduction	Last week, we introduced the concept of having a moral code. Today we are going to dig deeper by taking a closer look at the moral code of TMP, known as the 5 Virtues. Today, we will begin with the first virtue: Love.
25 mins	**Lesson**	Most of this lesson will be spent exploring what ideas and notions you already have about the concepts of love. The rest of the session will be

"Manhood is about being present, not perfect." –Phil Black

		reserved for sharing and learning perspectives from one another. 1. Give each student a "What is Love?" worksheet. 2. Allow 15 to 20 minutes for completion. 3. Once finished, ask for volunteers to share their answers. 4. Ask questions for clarity (when needed) and challenge when appropriate. *Reminder: The goal is not to dismiss innate ideas or to force them to take on any particular point of view, but rather to guide their thinking and introduce alternative perspectives.*
25 mins	**Close**	Post-Assessment: Have students complete the post assessment (6 mins) Clean-up (4 mins) Reflection (10 mins) Closing points: ❑ The word love has many meanings. The definition changes depending on who you refer to. ❑ Today's session was designed to make you think about those various definitions and to challenge you to become aware of how and when you actually apply them. ❑ In order for someone to know that you love them, they not only have to hear it, they have to see, and feel it. ❑ That goes for your family, friends, community, and most importantly- yourself. ❑ How do you know that you truly love yourself- if you never say it to yourself or see it when you look in the mirror? What if you fail to see it within your behavior, how treat your body or in the pride you've taken to accomplish your goals? ❑ This is why Love is the first virtue. You have to learn to love yourself first, before you can truly love others. Announcements (2 mins) Parting Pledge (2 mins)

"Manhood is about being present, not perfect." –Phil Black

Session 36 What is Love Worksheet

This exercise is designed to help you explore your thoughts around the concepts of love, what it means to you and how you apply that definition to your life. Answer all questions completely and honestly.

1. In your own words, what is love?

2. How do you show love to:
   a. Mom/Dad/Guardian

   b. Friends

   c. Others

3. What does it mean to have self-love?

4. How do you show love to yourself?

5. How would someone else recognize that you love yourself? (Examples: Through talking to you? Observing your appearance and behavior? Learning about how you treat others? Seeing how much time you put into personal self-improvement.)

6. What are other ways to express how you love:
   a. Yourself?

   b. Your family?

   c. Your community?

Session 36 Post Assessment

1. What does it mean to have love:
   a. of self

   b. for family and friends

   c. for your community

2. Why is it so important to love yourself?

3. What does the statement "You don't have to hate yourself, to love others" mean to you?

"Manhood is about being present, not perfect." –Phil Black

SESSION 37: Respect

Unit 5   S37: Session Objectives

By the end of this session the learner will be able to:

1. Discuss what it means to be respected.

2. Share ways to earn respect.

3. Express what it means to be disrespectful and feel disrespected.

4. Communicate how showing respect towards others can increase the likelihood of receiving respect in return.

AGENDA

1. Sign-in

2. Snack & Chat

3. Welcome

4. Pre Assessment (optional)

5. Warm-up

6. Session Introduction
   - ❏ Overview
   - ❏ Objectives
   - ❏ Agenda

7. Lesson
   - ❏ Activity
   - ❏ Recap
   - ❏ Norms
   - ❏ Expectations

8. Close
   - ❏ Clean-up
   - ❏ Reflection
   - ❏ Announcements
   - ❏ Parting Pledge

"Manhood is about being present, not perfect." –Phil Black

ACTIVITIES
Movie: *ESPN's 30 for 30 "Benji" (The Ben Wilson Story)* *0:00:00 through 0:45:50 minutes

ROOM SET-UP	MATERIALS NEEDED
Full or Half Circle Seating	1. Flipchart Paper 2. Dry Erase Board 3. AV Equipment 4. Internet Access to Youtube 5. Benji Reflection I 6. Markers 7. Pens

SESSION PREP

1. Ensure sign-in sheet is available.

2. Print:

   ❏ Pre and post assessments
   ❏ Benji Worksheet I

3. Set-up transition music.

4. Make sure snacks are ready for distribution.

5. Write and post: Objectives, Agenda, Norms & Expectations, and Review Questions on separate sheets of flipchart paper. *If Dry Erase Board is available, use it to write session objectives. Reserve flipchart for the other information.*

6. Set up all AV equipment.

7. Ensure the video is loaded and ready to play.

"Manhood is about being present, not perfect." –Phil Black

SESSION DETAILS		
1.5 - 2 hr		
	Pre-Session	Set up all materials and music.
3 mins	**Sign-in**	Have students sign in as they enter the designated space.
15 mins	**Snack & Chat**	
3 mins	**Welcome**	Thank students for coming and introduce the warm-up
(optional)	**Highlights and Do-Overs**	
	Review	
8 mins	**Warm-up**	(Optional)
6 mins	**Pre Assessment**	(Optional)
	Introduction	
	Break	
	Session Introduction	❑ Over the next three sessions, we are going to deal with the concept of Respect- which is our second virtue. ❑ *Ask*: Who can tell me what respect is? How would you define it? **Expect, in many cases, the learners to describe feelings of respect and situations where respect is present or absent.* ❑ Respect is one of those words or concepts that may be difficult to define, but easy to describe. The reason, while we may not always have the language to share an exact definition- in most cases, we are fully aware of what it feels like when we are being shown both respect and disrespect. ❑ To aide in our understanding of this multi-layer concept, we are going to look at the life of a former star basketball player by the name of Ben "Benji" Wilson. Over the next few sessions, through the ESPN 30 for 30 documentary, we are going to breakdown the concept of respect. There are many lessons to draw from Ben

"Manhood is about being present, not perfect." –Phil Black

		Wilson's story, but our focus will be to further understand respect. Specifically: ❏ How is it earned? ❏ What does it look and feel like (from family, friends, community and ourselves). We will also discuss disrespect and the potential problems that often occur when we or another person feels disrespected.
46 mins	**Lesson**	The first part of today's documentary will focus on Ben, and his journey to become a highly recruited high school basketball player. After the video, we will have a short break, followed by a few questions to start our discussion. 1. Play the video from beginning through the 0:45:50 stopping point.
8 min	**Break**	
26 mins	**Lesson cont'd**	2. Give each student a "Benji I" worksheet. 3. Allow 10 to 15 minutes for completion. 4. Once finished, ask for volunteers to share their answers. (16 mins) 5. Ask questions for clarification (as needed) and challenge when appropriate. Reminder: The goal is not to dismiss ideas or to force them to take on any particular viewpoint, but to guide their thinking and introduce alternative perspectives.
25 mins	**Close**	Post-Assessment: Have students complete the post assessment (6 mins) Clean-up (4 mins) Reflection: (10 mins) ❏ Looking at the life of Ben Wilson, you can easily see that he was very well respected by his family, friends, and community. Thinking of how he acknowledged his brother by placing the medal around his neck, you can see that he had respect for others. Lastly, when you consider the amount of dedication and determination Ben demonstrated in working to become the best, we also may conclude that he had respect for himself. Announcements (2 mins) Parting Pledge (2 mins)

"Manhood is about being present, not perfect." –Phil Black

Session 37 Benji Worksheet I

1. How would you describe Ben "Benji" Wilson as a person and as a basketball player?

2. Would you say that Benji was well respected? Why or Why not?

3. What did people admire about Wilson?

4. How did Ben respond to not seeing his name ranked amongst the best players?

5. Describe how Ben Wilson felt about himself.

6. What lessons can you take from Benji based on what you know of him thus far?

"Manhood is about being present, not perfect." –Phil Black

SESSION 38: Respect (Part II)

U5.S38: Session Objectives

By the end of this session the learner will be able to:

1. Discuss what it means to be respected.

2. Share ways to earn respect.

3. Express what it means to be both disrespected and disrespectful.

4. Communicate how showing respect towards others can increase the likelihood of receiving respect in return.

AGENDA

1. Sign-in

2. Snack & Chat

3. Welcome

4. Pre Assessment (optional)

5. Warm-up

6. Session Introduction
   - ❏ Overview
   - ❏ Objectives
   - ❏ Agenda

7. Lesson
   - ❏ Activity
   - ❏ Recap
   - ❏ Norms
   - ❏ Expectations

8. Close
   - ❏ Clean-up
   - ❏ Reflection
   - ❏ Announcements
   - ❏ Parting Pledge

"Manhood is about being present, not perfect." –Phil Black

ACTIVITIES
1. Warm-up: "You Trippin" 2. Movie: *ESPN's 30 for 30 "Benji" (The Ben Wilson Story)* *Starting at 0:45:50

ROOM SET-UP	MATERIALS NEEDED
Full or Half Circle Seating	1. Flipchart Paper 2. Dry Erase Board 3. AV Equipment 4. Internet Access to Youtube 5. Markers 6. Pens

SESSION PREP

1. Ensure sign-in sheet is ready.

2. Print:
   ❏ Pre and post assessments

3. Set-up transition music.

4. Make sure snacks are ready to distribute.

5. Write and post: Objectives, Agenda, Norms & Expectations, and Review Questions on separate sheets of flipchart paper. *If Dry Erase Board is available, use it to write session objectives. Reserve flipchart for the other information.*

6. Set up AV equipment.

7. Ensure the video is loaded and ready to play at the 0:45:50 min mark.

"Manhood is about being present, not perfect." –Phil Black

SESSION DETAILS		
1.5 - 2 hr		
	Pre-Session	Set up all materials and music.
3 mins	**Sign-in**	Have students sign in as they enter the designated space.
15 mins	**Snack & Chat**	
3 mins	**Welcome**	Thank students for coming and introduce the warm-up
(optional)	**Highlights and Do-Overs**	
	Review	
8 mins	**Warm-up: You trippin!**	1. Separate the group into smaller, equal groups of 3 or more. 2. Instruct them to: ❏ Create a skit of someone being disrespectful. This can be a reenactment of a member's experience or completely fictional. ❏ Prepare the group to demonstrate the incident and then explain how it was resolved. If there was no resolution, be prepared to share why. ❏ Allow 8-10 minutes for planning and 2 - 4 minutes for each skit (depending on the size of the group). 3. After each group has presented, thank them and move to the next part of the session.
6 mins	**Pre Assessment**	
	Introduction	
	Break	
	Session Introduction	❏ We are discussing the concept of respect by looking at the life of Ben Wilson.

"Manhood is about being present, not perfect." –Phil Black

		❏ Today we'll continue Ben's story, but transition our focus a bit. ❏ Like the warm-up suggested, we are going to discuss our perceptions regarding disrespect. ❏ Unlike last week, the video will be stopped as we go along, for dialogue and questions. The first stopping point will come fairly quickly. ❏ Ask if there are any questions before beginning, then start the video.

25 mins	**Lesson**	❏ In this segment, we will learn more about Benji and his relationship with his girlfriend. There will be a lot of topics and even questions that may come up outside of our focus. I ask that you write them down and hold them until later. *Play clip beginning at 0:45:50*
		
		Stopping point 1: 0:48:26
		
		Discussion Questions:
		
		    1. Explain what just happened?
		
		    2. What is the reason that Ben pushed his teacher?
		
		    3. What was he originally angry about?
		
		    4. Can someone share a time, when they were angry at someone or something but took it out someone else? (take1-3 responses)
		
		    5. How do you think his teacher felt?
		
		While you may see some elements of respect and disrespect within this next segment, the intent is to:
		
		1. Give you a complete picture of Ben Wilson's experience.
		
		2. Prepare you for the larger discussion on this topic, which is found later in the video.
		
		Continue the clip
		Note: *Because of the emotional content featured in the next segment, a brief break is recommended (at the 0:58:27 mark) for processing.*

		Stopping point 2: Discussion Question: In recognition of the emotions created by that last portion, I want to take a moment to simply ask if anyone has any questions or comments they would like to ask or share? *Answer questions and respond to comments when needed. Allow space for participants to share their thoughts or questions. *Continue the video Stopping point 3: 1:11:19mins Discussion Questions: 1. Though they were doing their jobs, how could someone perceive the media's behavior as disrespectful? 2. What personal lessons can we draw from their example? 3. Why did some feel disrespected by the service to honor Ben? *Answer questions and respond to comments when needed. Allow space for participants to share their thoughts on questions that arise as well.
25 mins	**Close**	Post-Assessment: Have students complete the post assessment (6 mins) Clean-up (4 mins) Reflection: (10 mins) ❑ In our remaining time, aside from what we are taking away from Ben's life on respect, what else have you learned? ❑ Next week, as we close out this session, we will get a chance to hear from the young man that assaulted Ben. In his conversation, you will have the opportunity to draw even more lessons. Announcements (2 mins) Parting Pledge (2 mins)

SESSION 39: Respect (Part III)

Unit 5   S39: Session Objectives

By the end of this session the learner will be able to:

1. Discuss what it means to be respected.

2. Share ways to earn respect.

3. Express what it means to be both disrespectful and disrespected.

4. Communicate how showing respect towards others can increase the likelihood of receiving respect in return.

AGENDA

1. Sign-in

2. Snack & Chat

3. Welcome

4. Pre Assessment (optional)

5. Warm-up

6. Session Introduction
   - ❑ Overview
   - ❑ Objectives
   - ❑ Agenda

7. Lesson
   - ❑ Activity
   - ❑ Recap
   - ❑ Norms
   - ❑ Expectations

8. Close
   - ❑ Clean-up
   - ❑ Reflection
   - ❑ Announcements
   - ❑ Parting Pledge

"Manhood is about being present, not perfect." –Phil Black

ACTIVITIES
Movie: *ESPN's 30 for 30 "Benji" (The Ben Wilson Story)* *1:11:19 through the end. 26 mins total.

ROOM SET-UP	MATERIALS NEEDED
Full or Half Circle Seating	1. Flipchart Paper 2. Dry Erase Board 3. AV Equipment 4. Internet Access to Youtube 5. Benji Reflection II 6. Markers 7. Pens

SESSION PREP

1. Ensure sign-in sheet is available.

2. Print:
   - ❏ Pre and post assessments
   - ❏ Benji Worksheet II

3. Set-up transition music.

4. Make sure snacks are ready to distribute.

5. Write and post Objectives, Agenda, Norms & Expectations and Review Questions on separate sheets of flipchart paper. *If Dry Erase Board is available, use it to write session objectives. Reserve flipchart for the other information.*

6. Set up AV equipment.

7. Ensure the video is loaded and ready to play through.

"Manhood is about being present, not perfect." –Phil Black

SESSION DETAILS		
1.5 - 2 hr		
	Pre-Session	Set up all materials and music.
3 mins	**Sign-in**	Have students sign in as they enter the designated space.
15 mins	**Snack & Chat**	
3 mins	**Welcome**	Thank students for coming and introduce the warm-up
(optional)	**Highlights and Do-Overs**	
	Review	
8 mins	**Warm-up**	Optional
6 mins	**Pre Assessment**	
	Introduction	
	Break	
	Session Introduction	Today we are going to close out our lesson on Respect, and the Ben Wilson Story. We will need a significant amount of time for reflection and discussion, so I will play the final 26 minutes uninterrupted. Please write down any questions or concerns, and we'll address them later.
25 mins	**Lesson**	In the final part of this documentary, we hear from Billy (the young man that assaulted Benji) regarding his side of the story. Once the video is complete, there will be a reflection and discussion. 1. Play the video from 1:11:19 through the end. 2. Give each student a "Benji II" worksheet. 3. Allow 15 to 20 minutes to complete. 4. Once finished, ask for volunteers to share their answers.

"Manhood is about being present, not perfect." –Phil Black

5. Ask questions for clarity when needed and challenge where appropriate.

Reminder: The goal is not to dismiss ideas or to force them to take on any particular point of view, but rather to guide their thinking and introduce them to alternative perspectives.

	Close	Post-Assessment: Have students complete the post assessment (6 mins) Clean-up (4 mins) Reflection: (10 mins) ❏ While there are many lessons and topics to withdraw from this discussion, one in particular is the irony that both young men crossed paths only because they were both dealing with situations that upset them causing them to deviate from their normal behavior or routines. For Benji it was the argument with his girlfriend. For Billy, it was hearing that someone had possibly stolen from his cousin. Announcements: (2 mins) ❏ "When you give respect, you are more likely to receive it," is not only a virtue of TMP and found within the description of Respect, it's also the main concept that we ultimately want you to walk away with. ❏ Ben Wilson was well respected by everyone, partly because he had a high regard for himself. That is why we declare in the TMP pledge "Respect must start from within, given and earned BEFORE it can be received." Parting Pledge (2 mins)

"Manhood is about being present, not perfect." –Phil Black

Session 39 Benji Worksheet II

1. How did the loss of his father affect Billy (the shooter)?

2. What was Billy and Omar's reason for going to Simeon High School?

3. "The issue of the stolen money had already been settled by the time Billy and Omar reached the school." Describe a time when you were ready to take action on behalf of someone else, only to find out later that the problem had been resolved. Or, the person continued to get into similar situations.

4. According to Billy's account of what took place, Ben shoved him out of the way without apologizing. Based on what we've seen from this documentary, regarding Ben's character, do you think Billy's account of what took place is consistent or different of Ben's behavior?

"Manhood is about being present, not perfect." –Phil Black

5. While the feeling of disrespect may have been natural for many in Billy's situation, what role do you feel having a gun played in his reaction? How do you think the situation would've unfolded had Billy been unarmed?

6. Think of a time when you over-reacted to a situation or someone being disrespectful towards you. Describe how you felt afterwards.

7. Explain your views of respect and disrespect as a result of seeing the Ben Wilson story. What changes will you make in your own personal life as a result?

"Manhood is about being present, not perfect." –Phil Black

Session 37/38/39 Post Assessment

1. What does it mean to be respected?

2. How does a person earn respect?

3. What life lessons did you take away from the Ben Wilson story?

4. How does showing respect increase the likelihood of receiving it?

SESSION 40: Courage, Provision, and Protection

Unit 5 S40: Session Objectives

By the end of this session the learner will be able to:

1. Define courage and what it means to be courageous.

2. Recognize the importance of building a foundation for the future.

3. Communicate ways to prepare for a strong family.

4. Explain why protecting those that are unable to protect themselves is a vital part of being a man.

AGENDA

1. Sign-in

2. Snack & Chat

3. Welcome

4. Pre Assessment (optional)

5. Warm-up

6. Session Introduction
   - ❑ Overview
   - ❑ Objectives
   - ❑ Agenda

7. Lesson
   - ❑ Activity
   - ❑ Recap
   - ❑ Norms
   - ❑ Expectations

8. Close
   - ❑ Clean-up
   - ❑ Reflection
   - ❑ Announcements
   - ❑ Parting Pledge

"Manhood is about being present, not perfect." –Phil Black

ACTIVITIES
1. Warm-Up: Tell me…
2. Group Presentations

ROOM SET-UP	MATERIALS NEEDED
Full or Half Circle Seating	1. Flipchart Paper 2. Dry Erase Board 3. Printing Paper 4. Markers 5. Pens

SESSION PREP

1. Ensure sign-in sheet is available.

2. Print:
   - ❑ Pre and post assessments
   - ❑ Copies of opening and closing pledge

3. Set-up transition music.

4. Make sure snacks are ready for distribution.

5. Write and post: Objectives, Agenda, Norms & Expectations, and Review Questions on separate sheets of flipchart paper. *If Dry Erase Board is available, use it to write session objectives. Reserve flipchart for the other information.*

6. Courage Provision Protection Presentation Questions

"Manhood is about being present, not perfect." –Phil Black

SESSION DETAILS

1.5 - 2 hr		
	Pre-Session	Set up all materials and music.
3 mins	**Sign-in**	Have students sign in as they enter the designated space.
15 mins	**Snack & Chat**	
3 mins	**Welcome**	Thank students for coming and introduce the warm-up
(optional)	**Highlights and Do-Overs**	
	Review	

8 mins	**Warm-up: "Tell me…"**	1. Instruct students to find a partner.
		
		2. *Say*: This is called "Tell me…"
		
		    ❑ I am going to call out a topic.
		
		    ❑ You will turn to your partner, asking them to share about themselves regarding the topic you suggest. Start by saying "Tell me…" (then repeat the topic in a manner that allows them to share).
		
		Examples:
		
		1. If I say: "video games" you could say: "tell me about a time you lost a close game that you should have won in 2K."
		
		2. Another example could be: If I say "candy," you may say: "tell me about your favorite candy."
		
		Note: Incorporate 2 - 3 random (light) topics of your own to start. Then move to the following topics. Have both partners give responses to the next three.
		
		Topics:
		
		1. Courage

"Manhood is about being present, not perfect." –Phil Black

		2. Provide 3. Protect *Ideally, students will discuss different times in their lives when they have displayed courage, had to provide for someone or protect another.* If discussions do not touch on these areas in some way, use the opportunity to pose direct questions during the lesson introduction. Example: "Someone tell me a time when they had to use courage."
6 mins	**Pre Assessment**	
	Introduction	
	Break	
	Session Introduction	❏ We'll close out our unit on the Five virtues today, by covering the last three, which are: Courage, Provision, and Protection. *Review TMP's interpretation of these three.* ❏ Not only is that TMP's interpretation, like the other virtues explained, that interpretation is an example for you to look towards and live by. ❏ I want to know what are your interpretations of these three virtues is. How do they manifest themselves in your lives? How do others perceive these virtues within you?
25 mins	**Lesson**	We are going to break up into three groups. Each group has a list of questions. Using your answers, you are going to create and share a group presentation. You can either do a traditional teach-back or something creative. The only requirements are: 1. There must be an identifiable introduction, body, and conclusion. 2. All questions must be addressed. 3. Everyone in the group must participate in the planning and presentation of your group's interpretations. Allow ❏ 15-20 minutes for planning ❏ 3-5 minutes per group for presentations

"Manhood is about being present, not perfect." –Phil Black

		At the conclusion of all presentations, ask questions for clarity (when needed) and challenge where appropriate.
		Reminder: The goal is not to dismiss ideas or to force them to take on any particular viewpoint, but rather to guide their thinking and introduce them to alternative perspectives
		Note: The objective of this lesson is to lay the foundation for students to think critically about their personal beliefs or moral code.
25 mins	**Close**	Post-Assessment: Have students complete the post assessment (6 mins)
		Clean-up (4 mins)
		Reflection (10 mins)
		❑ We are going to have our unit assessment, but I would like to ask for feedback on what you've learned. How does having a moral code, like the 5 Virtues, help you as a man?
		Announcements (2 mins)
		Parting Pledge (2 mins)

Session 40 Courage, Provision, Protection Presentation Questions

<u>Courage Questions</u>

1. What is courage?

2. Why is it important to be courageous?

3. How would a man without courage be viewed by others?

4. Share an example of a time when you were courageous. Include your emotions as well as those of the person that benefited from your act of courage.

5. Do you feel that all men should display courage? Why or why not?

"Manhood is about being present, not perfect." –Phil Black

Provision Presentation Questions

1. What does it mean to provide?

2. Why is it important to for a man to be in a position to provide for himself as well as his family?

3. How does a young person begin to build a sound foundation that will ensure they are able to provide for their future?

4. What could be the consequences for a young person, If he does not properly lay down a foundation to provide for himself, and his family, early on in life?

5. How do you plan to continue laying a foundation that will allow you to provide for yourself and others?

"Manhood is about being present, not perfect." –Phil Black

Protection Presentation Questions

1. What does it mean to protect?

2. Why is protecting yourself and others important?

3. How would you view a man who was unwilling to protect himself, his family or those that are unable to defend themselves?

4. Share an example of a time when you had to protect someone. Include how it felt for you (and the person that benefited from your protection).

5. Do you feel all men should be a protector? Why or why not?

"Manhood is about being present, not perfect." –Phil Black

SESSION 41: Assessment, Recognition, and Reflection

Unit 5   S41: Session Objectives

By the end of this session the learner will be able to:

1. Identify the most impactful aspects of Unit V.

2. Share any changes made since the first session.

3. Recognize students that have made improvements.

4. Set goals for the next unit.

AGENDA

1. Sign-in

2. Welcome

3. Q & A

4. Unit Assessment

5. Reactions

6. Recognition

7. Reflection

8. Unit IV Overview

9. Close
   - ❑ Clean-up
   - ❑ Announcements
   - ❑ Parting Pledge

"Manhood is about being present, not perfect." –Phil Black

ACTIVITIES
1. Unit Assessment 2. Games

ROOM SET-UP	MATERIALS NEEDED
Full or Half Circle Seating	1. Unit Assessment 2. Certificates & Awards (Unit V Completion, Most Improved, and Man of the Month). 3. Dry Erase Board 4. Markers 5. Pens

SESSION PREP
1. Print Unit Assessments. 2. Set-up transition music. 3. Purchase special meal to celebrate.

"Manhood is about being present, not perfect." –Phil Black

SESSION DETAILS		
1.5 - 2 hr		
	Pre-Session	Set up all materials and music.
3 mins	**Sign-in**	Have students sign in as they enter the designated space.
3 mins	**Welcome**	Thank students for coming and give an overview of the day
(optional)	**Highlights and Do-Overs**	
8 mins	**Q&A**	Answer any questions about the material from the previous sessions
25 mins	**Unit Assessment**	Administer assessment
6 mins	**Break**	
5 mins	**Reactions**	Any thoughts about the test?
20 mins	**Recognition**	Share words of encouragement- while recognizing each individual and their personal progress.
3 mins	**Reflection**	What part of Unit V has left the biggest impact on you? What personal changes have you made since beginning this project?
8 mins	**Unit VI Overview**	
5 mins	**Break**	
8 mins	**Close**	Clean-up (4 mins) Announcements (2 mins) Parting Pledge (2 mins)

"Manhood is about being present, not perfect." –Phil Black

Unit 6: Discipline, Self-Guidance, and Leadership

"Service to others is the rent you pay for your room here on earth."
-Muhammad Ali

"Manhood is about being present, not perfect." –Phil Black

Unit 6 Background and Overview

The final unit concludes by reiterating lessons and experiences previously learned throughout the curriculum. This unit not only covers review, it also assists the student in application of previous material for everyday life. Unit 6 is extremely essential, as it also yields important tools for the students to manifest the Five Virtues, while continually increasing their self-awareness learned from the previous five units.

The curriculum guide closes with these particular lessons, so that students can have a basic understanding of what they've learned and how it can be incorporated into their lives, starting the day they finish the TMP, through adulthood.

Two lesson plans are open at the end for year-end celebrations, recognition, awards, and activity days.

Here's a list of the sessions included within this unit:

SESSION 42:   Guest Speaker
SESSION 43:   Student 1:1s and Self-Care
SESSION 44:   My Journey
SESSION 45:   Leadership
SESSION 46:   Motivation 101
SESSION 47:   Inspiration
SESSION 48:   Plan Your Own Lesson
SESSION 49:   Plan Your Own Lesson

"Manhood is about being present, not perfect." –Phil Black

"Manhood is about being present, not perfect." –Phil Black

SESSION 42: Guest Speaker

For Guest Speaker Lesson templates, please visit the Resource section

"Manhood is about being present, not perfect." –Phil Black

SESSION 43: Student One-on-Ones

For One-on-One Lesson templates, please visit the Resource section

"Manhood is about being present, not perfect." –Phil Black

SESSION 44: My Journey

Unit 6   S44: Session Objectives

By the end of this session the learner will be able to:

1. Discuss positive changes and progress made since beginning the program.

2. Share personal stories of praise from others that have noticed growth and improvement.

3. Set at least one goal to be accomplished after the program has concluded.

AGENDA

1. Sign-in

2. Snack & Chat

3. Welcome

4. Pre Assessment (optional)

5. Warm-up

6. Session Introduction
   - ❏ Overview
   - ❏ Objectives
   - ❏ Agenda

7. Lesson
   - ❏ Activity
   - ❏ Recap
   - ❏ Norms
   - ❏ Expectations

8. Close
   - ❏ Clean-up
   - ❏ Reflection
   - ❏ Announcements
   - ❏ Parting Pledge

"Manhood is about being present, not perfect." –Phil Black

ACTIVITIES

1. Warm-Up: Discussion
2. My Journey

ROOM SET-UP	MATERIALS NEEDED
Full or Half Circle Seating	1. Flipchart Paper 2. Dry Erase Board 3. My Journey Worksheets A & B 4. Markers 5. Pens

SESSION PREP

1. Ensure sign-in sheet is available.

2. Print:
   - ❑ Pre and post assessments
   - ❑ My Journey Worksheets

3. Set-up transition music.

4. Make sure snacks are ready for distribution.

5. *Write* and post: Objectives, Agenda, Norms & Expectations and Review Questions on separate sheets of flipchart paper. *If Dry Erase Board is available, use it to write session objectives. Reserve flipchart for the other information.*

"Manhood is about being present, not perfect." –Phil Black

SESSION DETAILS		
1.5 - 2 hr		
	Pre-Session	Set up all materials and music.
3 mins	**Sign-in**	Have students sign in as they enter the designated space.
8 mins	**Snack & Chat**	
3 mins	**Welcome**	Thank students for coming and introduce the warm-up
(optional)	**Highlights and Do-Overs**	
	Review	
20-30 mins	**Warm-up**	❑ We have been working together for several weeks. ❑ Many of you (or all of you) have made significant strides in one or more areas. Question: What changes or areas of growth are you most proud of? *Allow time for each participant to share.* Question: Who can share a recent compliment or even praise, that they've received from someone- as a result of personal changes (such as: behavior, attitude, decision making...etc) that they've made?
6 mins	**Pre Assessment**	
	Introduction	
	Break	
	Session Introduction	❑ As the program begins to come to an end, it is important that we acknowledge and celebrate our progress. ❑ It is equally (if not more) important, that we continue to challenge ourselves to move forward. ❑ Today we are going to do that by setting a developmental goal- to accomplish going into next school year.

"Manhood is about being present, not perfect." –Phil Black

| 25 mins | **Lesson** | The worksheet that you'll receive today is called: My Journey. This worksheet is designed to help you as you set personal goals.

Give students the option of completing the worksheet as an entire group or individually.

Once completed, allow time for sharing and discussion. |
| --- | --- | --- |
| 25 mins | **Close** | Post-Assessment:
Have students complete the post assessment (6 mins)

Clean-up (4 mins)

Reflection (10 mins)

Announcements: (2 mins)
*For next session, think about someone you know personally (or a celebrity) that you feel exemplifies what it means to be a leader. Be ready to discuss that person.

Parting Pledge (2 mins) |

"Manhood is about being present, not perfect." –Phil Black

Session 44 My Journey - Part A

_____'s Journey

My Personal Goal

The Manhood Project (TMP) is a mentoring program designed to help boys develop into successful young men and leaders. For this to happen, each participant must be committed to his own development. The TMP program offers guidance and support, but you have to do the work to yield results. Congratulations on making it this far into the program. The next step is to set personal goals for yourself as you continue moving forward.

Problem or Personal Challenge

To set a goal we sometimes have to start with a problem or personal challenge within our lives. Think about an area of your life or specific behavior that you are still having difficulties in, and write it down.

Follow up questions: How is this a problem for you? Describe what is happening as a result of your continued struggle. How is it affecting your relationships with your parents, siblings, friends and/or teachers?

What are the potential dangers if this problem or challenge continues?

"Manhood is about being present, not perfect." –Phil Black

If continued, how might this problem/challenge affect your life in the next:
Week?

Month?

Year?

Forever?

"Manhood is about being present, not perfect." –Phil Black

Session 43 My Journey - Part B

Setting Your Goal

Now that you have acknowledged the problem, you are in a better position to set and achieve your goals.

Examples: By the time we return to school next fall, I will:
Be able to control my attitude.
Show more confidence in myself.
Demonstrate better study habits.

By the next school year I will:

The following questions will help clarify your goal:

1. Describe how you will:
   a. **Look** when you meet your goal. How will you view yourself physically?

   How will others view you?

   b. **Sound** when you meet your goal. What words or phrases will you hear from yourself?

   What will you hear from others about you?

"Manhood is about being present, not perfect." –Phil Black

c. **Feel** when you meet your goal. How will you feel in your body?

What might others feel in their bodies when interacting with you?

How will you feel about yourself overall? (Explain)

How might others feel about you as a person? (Explain)

d. **Do** when you meet your goal. What behaviors/actions will you engage in?

What will others see you doing consistently?

2. When do you want to have this goal met? Be specific.

"Manhood is about being present, not perfect." –Phil Black

3. How will you know that you have met your goal?
   I will know that I have met my goal when (explain):

4. List the people who will be affected by you meeting this goal.
   - ❏
   - ❏
   - ❏
   - ❏
   - ❏
   - ❏
   - ❏
   - ❏
   - ❏

5. Describe (in at least two) ways, in which they will be affected.

6. How will accomplishing this goal affect other areas of your life?

"Manhood is about being present, not perfect." –Phil Black

SESSION 45: Leadership

Unit 6   S45: Session Objectives

By the end of this session the learner will be able to:

1. Define leadership.

2. Identify examples of positive and poor leaders.

3. Determine what type of leader they want to be.

4. Express the steps needed to take on the characteristics of a leader.

AGENDA

1. Sign-in

2. Snack & Chat

3. Welcome

4. Pre Assessment (optional)

5. Warm-up

6. Session Introduction
   - ❑ Overview
   - ❑ Objectives
   - ❑ Agenda

7. Lesson
   - ❑ Activity
   - ❑ Recap
   - ❑ Norms
   - ❑ Expectations

8. Close
   - ❑ Clean-up
   - ❑ Reflection
   - ❑ Announcements
   - ❑ Parting Pledge

"Manhood is about being present, not perfect." –Phil Black

ACTIVITIES

1. Warm-up: Who's the Leader?
2. Discussion
3. Leadership worksheet

ROOM SET-UP	MATERIALS NEEDED
Full or Half Circle Seating	1. Flipchart Paper 2. Index Cards 3. Dry Erase Board 4. Leadership worksheet 5. Markers 6. Pens

SESSION PREP

1. Ensure sign-in sheet is ready.

2. Print:
   ❑ Pre and post assessments
   ❑ Copies Leadership Worksheet

3. Set-up transition music.

4. Make sure snacks are ready to distribute.

5. Write and post: Objectives, Agenda, Norms & Expectations, and Review Questions on separate sheets of flipchart paper. *If Dry Erase Board is available, use it to write session objectives. Reserve flipchart for the other information.*

6. Predetermine the number of small groups (3-5) you will have for the second activity.
   a. Prepare one sheet of flipchart for each group by:
      i. Drawing a vertical line down the center.
      ii. Write "Good" at the top of the paper on the left side of the line.
      iii. Write "Bad" at the top of the paper on the right side of the line.

"Manhood is about being present, not perfect." –Phil Black

SESSION DETAILS		
1.5 - 2 hr		
	Pre-Session	Set up all materials and music.
3 mins	**Sign-in**	Have students sign in as they enter the designated space.
8 mins	**Snack & Chat**	
3 mins	**Welcome**	Thank students for coming and introduce the warm-up
(optional)	**Highlights and Do-Overs**	
	Review	
5-15 mins	**Warm-up: Who's the Leader?[3]**	1. Choose one person to be "it," and leave the room. 2. Choose a second person to lead the remaining players sitting (or standing) in a circle. 3. The person leading the players starts a simple motion that everyone else follows together, such as: slapping hands against the knees, and then changes the motions periodically. 4. Direct players (before "It" returns) to avoid staring at the leader and revealing his identity. 5. When "It" returns, have "It" stand in the center of the circle. He'll now have three guesses to try and name the leader. 6. If "it" guesses correctly, the leader becomes the new "It." If the guess is incorrect, "It" will remain for another round. Reflection Questions: ❏ How challenging was it to be the leader? ❏ How challenging was it to be part of the group without giving the leader away?

---

[3] Great Group Games, by Susan Ragsdale and Ann Saylor

"Manhood is about being present, not perfect." –Phil Black

		❏ How challenging was it to be "It?" ❏ What happens when a leader gives conflicting instructions? (We will revisit this question later)
6 mins	**Pre Assessment**	
	Introduction	
	Break	
	Session Introduction	In the last session, we asked that you come prepared to talk about someone you view as a leader. Today, we will focus on the leader you've chosen and the concept of leadership. *Ask*: What is a leader? **Example Target: Someone who guides others.* A leader guides people in many ways. To be an effective team leader in life, we must first recognize what it takes to be a good leader.
25 mins	**Lesson**	Activity two ❏ Using an index card, write on one side everything that you admire about the person you've identified as a good leader. (Allow 3-5 minutes) -Once everyone has finished, have students briefly talk about the person they've selected. (10-15 minutes) ❏ Now, consider the worst example of a leader that you can think of. Using the back of the same index card, describe what makes that person a bad example of a leader -without using their name. (Allow 3-5 minutes) -Once everyone has finished writing, split students into 3 - 4 equal small groups. ❏ Using the flip chart, write all of the qualities (good and bad) that were identified by the students. Place a checkmark next to any duplicates. (Allow 6 -10 minutes) Once complete, have the groups share out loud. (10 minutes) *The main point of this activity is to uncover the most consistent attributes of a leader.*

"Manhood is about being present, not perfect." –Phil Black

	Break	
30 mins	**Close**	Post-Assessment: Have students complete the post assessment (6 mins)
		Clean-up (4 mins)
		Reflection (15 mins) Have students complete the leadership handout. If time permits, allow them to share their answers with the group.
		Closing: During the warm-up, we posed the question: "What happens when a leader gives conflicting instructions?" There are many points to that question. The main point being: the need to be consistent as a leader. Consistent in not only your mind- but your language and actions count just as much. When any of these components are out of alignment, it reduces our effectiveness as leaders.
		Announcements (2 mins)
		Parting Pledge (2 mins)

"Manhood is about being present, not perfect." –Phil Black

SESSION 46: Motivation 101

Unit 6   S46: Session Objectives

By the end of this session the learner will be able to:

1. Reflect on the people and events (past or present) that are most important to them and the impact they have made.

2. Communicate the difference between: Motivation and Inspiration.

3. Develop a why statement.

4. Recognize how to use their "why" as motivation to excel.

AGENDA

1. Sign-in

2. Snack & Chat

3. Welcome

4. Warm-up

5. Pre Assessment (optional)

6. Session Introduction
   - ❑ Overview
   - ❑ Objectives
   - ❑ Agenda

7. Lesson
   - ❑ Define Terms
   - ❑ What and/or Who (reflection)
   - ❑ From Pain to Power (developing a why)
   - ❑ Using your why

8. Close
   - ❑ Clean-up
   - ❑ Reflection
   - ❑ Announcements
   - ❑ Parting Pledge

"Manhood is about being present, not perfect." –Phil Black

ACTIVITIES

1. Warm-Up: Poem "*If*" and Discussion
2. What (events) and/or Who (has impacted your life)
3. "*Why*" Video: https://youtu.be/JXTfho6yo9g

ROOM SET-UP	MATERIALS NEEDED
Full or Half Circle Seating	1. Poem "*If*" 2. Loose paper 3. AV Equipment 4. Access to YouTube 5. Dry Erase Board 6. Printing Paper 7. Markers 8. Pens

SESSION PREP

1. Ensure sign-in sheet is available.

2. Set-up transition music.

3. Make sure snacks are ready for distribution.

4. Write and post: Objectives and Agenda on separate sheets of flipchart paper. *If Dry Erase Board is available, use it to write session objectives. Reserve flipchart for the other information.*

5. Print copies of the poem.

"Manhood is about being present, not perfect." –Phil Black

1.5 - 2 hr		
	Pre-Session	Set up all materials and music.
3 mins	**Sign-in**	Have students sign in as they enter the designated space.
8 mins	**Snack & Chat**	
3 mins	**Welcome**	Thank students for coming and introduce the warm-up
(optional)	**Highlights and Do-Overs**	
	Review	

8 mins	**Warm-up: Scenario Worksheets**	*Say*: Today's session will start with a poem that we'll read together as a group.
		
		(Pass out copies)
		
		Post questions
		    1. What initial feelings or thoughts come to mind after reading this?
		
		    2. What line stands out to you the most?
		
		Say: This poem was read to get your thoughts flowing before we went into the actual lesson. However, we will revisit this at the end if there is time.
		
		For now, let's move on.

6 mins	**Pre Assessment**	
5 mins	**Session Introduction**	Today we are going to talk about possibly the most critical tool in becoming a leader and growing as a person: Motivation. Can someone read our objectives? Objectives: Have a volunteer read the objectives. Provide any clarity you feel is

"Manhood is about being present, not perfect." –Phil Black

		needed.
		Agenda: After the objectives have been covered, reveal and recite the agenda.
25 mins	**Lesson**	Define Terms: (4 mins) Write the word: "Inspiration" and ask: 1. Can someone tell me what this means? *Target answer: A feeling that you get from a person or thing, that moves you into action.* Write the word "Motivation" next to it and ask: 1. What is Motivation? *Target: (If needed, use the root word Motive) A reason for doing something.* 2. What separates the two? *Target: Inspiration is external (meaning you get it from others or other things), while motivation is internal.* Today we are going to focus on the internal. To get us started, we are going to take a few minutes to simply relax. *Do a 3-5 minute meditation to music. At the end, the Facilitator shares a personal story about the person or event that drives them to be successful. Facilitator ends by stating: "That is what (or who) is significant to me." *Say:* For the next part of our session, we would like for you to take some time to reflect and identify what person or event is most significant to you. Using a sheet of paper: We want you to either: (1) list the people in your life that have helped you in some significant way. Or :(2) write about an event that has shaped who you are. Take 10-12 minutes.
	Break	
		❑ Discussion: Who wants to share their list? ❑ Pain to Power A poet and artist by the name of Anthony Beady often talks about transforming pain into power. As a leader you have to learn this incredible skill, because it can make all of the difference in being

"Manhood is about being present, not perfect." –Phil Black

		an exceptional leader. One way to do this is by using the people or events in your life as the "Why" behind your actions. ❏ Play the "*Why*" video ❏ Facilitator relates their personal story to their "Why." Example: "Since I know what it is like to grow up without a father, I chose to do something in my life to help those like me." That's what drives me every day.
25 mins	**Close**	Post-Assessment: Have students complete the post assessment. (6 mins) Clean-up (4 mins) Reflection (10 mins) Encourage students to write a "why" statement by simply declaring their personal reason to remain committed to being their best selves. For those who may need more time to process, allow them to share during next session. Announcements: (2 mins) Now that we know the difference between motivation and inspiration, for next week I want you to bring in something that inspires you. It can be a picture, poem, song, video clip or something that you wish to talk about. Parting Pledge (2 mins)

"Manhood is about being present, not perfect." –Phil Black

Session 46 *If* by Rudyard Kipling

If by Rudyard Kipling

If you can keep your head when all about you
 Are losing theirs and blaming it on you,
If you can trust yourself when all men doubt you,
 But make allowance for their doubting too;
If you can wait and not be tired by waiting,
 Or being lied about, don't deal in lies,
Or being hated, don't give way to hating,
 And yet don't look too good, nor talk too wise:

If you can dream- and not make dreams your master;
 If you can think- and not make thoughts your aim;
If you can meet with Triumph and Disaster
 And treat those two impostors just the same;
If you can bear to hear the truth you've spoken
 Twisted by knaves to make a trap for fools,
Or watch the things you gave your life to, broken,
 And stoop and build 'em up with worn-out tools:

If you can make one heap of all your winnings
 And risk it on one turn of pitch-and-toss,
And lose, and start again at your beginnings
 And never breathe a word about your loss;
If you can force your heart and nerve and sinew
 To serve your turn long after they are gone,
And so hold on when there is nothing in you
 Except the Will which says to them: "Hold on!"

If you can talk with crowds and keep your virtue,
 Or walk with Kings- nor lose the common touch,
If neither foes nor loving friends can hurt you,
 If all men count with you, but none too much;
If you can fill the unforgiving minute
 With sixty seconds' worth of distance run,
Yours is the Earth and everything that's in it,
 And- which is more- you'll be a Man, my son.

"Manhood is about being present, not perfect." –Phil Black

SESSION 47: Inspiration

Unit 6   S46: Session Objectives

By the end of this session the learner will be able to:

1. Share who or what inspires them.

2. Create a vision board. (If time permits)

3. Communicate how they will use what they have learned to inspire others.

AGENDA

1. Sign-in

2. Snack & Chat

3. Welcome

4. Pre Assessment (optional)

5. Warm-up

6. Session Introduction
   - ❏ Overview
   - ❏ Objectives
   - ❏ Agenda

7. Lesson
   - ❏ Activity
   - ❏ Recap
   - ❏ Norms
   - ❏ Expectations

8. Close
   - ❏ Clean-up
   - ❏ Reflection
   - ❏ Announcements
   - ❏ Parting Pledge

"Manhood is about being present, not perfect." –Phil Black

ACTIVITIES

1. Warm-up: I'm Inspired by…
2. Vision Board (optional)
3. Discussion

ROOM SET-UP	MATERIALS NEEDED
Full or Half Circle Seating	1. Flipchart Paper 2. Dry Erase Board 3. Printing Paper 4. Poster-boards (for all students) 5. Various images, words, statements (to be used for a vision board) 6. AV Equipment 7. Access to Youtube 8. Markers 9. Pens 10. An example of what inspires you 11. An Inspirational video or poem (for closing)

SESSION PREP

1. Ensure sign-in sheet is available.

2. Print:
   ❑ Pre and post assessments
   ❑ Words of affirmation on slips of paper

3. Set-up transition music.

4. Make sure snacks are ready for distribution.

5. Write and post: Objectives, Agenda, Norms & Expectations, and Review Questions on separate sheets of flipchart paper. *If Dry Erase Board is available, use it to write session objectives. Reserve flipchart for the other information.*

6. Set up AV Equipment.

7. Place clippings, images, words of affirmation, etc. on a table.

"Manhood is about being present, not perfect." –Phil Black

SESSION DETAILS		
1.5 - 2 hr		
	Pre-Session	Set up all materials and music.
3 mins	**Sign-in**	Have students sign in as they enter the designated space.
8 mins	**Snack & Chat**	
3 mins	**Welcome**	Thank students for coming and introduce the warm-up
(optional)	**Highlights and Do-Overs**	
	Review	
35 -45 mins	**Warm-up: I am inspired by**	❏ Have students to randomly share one by one- the image, poem, song, etc. that inspires them. ❏ Allow time for questions and discussion. ❏ Give relevant feedback and offer encouragement when appropriate.
6 mins	**Pre Assessment**	
	Introduction	
	Break	
	Session Introduction	A great tool that helps to bring daily inspiration is a vision board.
35 mins	**Lesson**	1. Instruct students to use the poster-boards, images, words, etc. to construct a visual representation of what they wish to accomplish in the future or how how they see themselves. 2. Have students share their Vision Boards. Provide relevant feedback
10 mins	**Close**	Post-Assessment: Have students complete the post assessment (6 mins)

"Manhood is about being present, not perfect." –Phil Black

Clean-up (4 mins)

Reflection (6 mins)
- ❏ *Ask*: How will you use what you have learned to inspire others?

- ❏ Play Inspirational clip or song that you've chosen

- ❏ Offer closing remarks and congratulations

Announcements (2 mins)

Parting Pledge (2 mins)

"Manhood is about being present, not perfect." –Phil Black

SESSION 48: Lesson Plan Template (Plan Your Own Session)

Unit 6   S47: Session Objectives
By the end of this session the learner will be able to: 1.
AGENDA

1. Sign-in

2. Snack & Chat

3. Welcome

4. Warm-up

5. Pre Assessment (optional)

6. Session Introduction
   - ❏ Overview
   - ❏ Objectives
   - ❏ Agenda

7. Lesson
   - ❏ Activity
   - ❏ Recap
   - ❏ Norms
   - ❏ Expectations

8. Close
   - ❏ Clean-up
   - ❏ Reflection
   - ❏ Announcements
   - ❏ Parting Pledge

"Manhood is about being present, not perfect." –Phil Black

ACTIVITIES

ROOM SET-UP	MATERIALS NEEDED
Full or Half Circle Seating	1. Flipchart Paper 2. Dry Erase Board 3. Printing Paper 4. Markers 5. Pens

SESSION PREP

1. Ensure sign-in sheet is ready.

2. Print:
   - Pre and post assessments
   - Copies of opening and closing pledge

3. Set-up transition music.

4. Make sure snacks are ready for distribution.

5. Write and post Objectives, Agenda, Norms & Expectations, and Review Questions on separate sheets of flipchart paper. *If Dry Erase Board is available, use it to write session objectives. Reserve flipchart for the other information.*

"Manhood is about being present, not perfect." –Phil Black

SESSION 49: Lesson Plan Template

Unit 6   S49: Session Objectives

By the end of this session the learner will be able to:
1.

AGENDA

1. Sign-in

2. Snack & Chat

3. Welcome

4. Warm-up

5. Pre Assessment (optional)

6. Session Introduction
   - ❏ Overview
   - ❏ Objectives
   - ❏ Agenda

7. Lesson
   - ❏ Activity
   - ❏ Recap
   - ❏ Norms
   - ❏ Expectations

8. Close
   - ❏ Clean-up
   - ❏ Reflection
   - ❏ Announcements
   - ❏ Parting Pledge

"Manhood is about being present, not perfect." –Phil Black

ACTIVITIES

ROOM SET-UP	MATERIALS NEEDED
Full or Half Circle Seating	1. Flipchart Paper 2. Dry Erase Board 3. Printing Paper 4. Markers 5. Pens

SESSION PREP

1. Ensure sign-in sheet is available.

2. Print:
   - ❏ Pre and post assessments
   - ❏ Copies of opening and closing pledge

3. Set-up transition music.

4. Make sure snacks are ready for distribution.

5. *Write* and post: Objectives, Agenda, Norms & Expectations, and Review Questions on separate sheets of flipchart paper. *If Dry Erase Board is available, use it to write session objectives. Reserve flipchart for the other information.*

"Manhood is about being present, not perfect." –Phil Black

		SESSION DETAILS
1.5 - 2 hr		
	Pre-Session	Set up all materials and music.
3 mins	**Sign-in**	Have students sign in as they enter the designated space.
15 mins	**Snack & Chat**	
3 mins	**Welcome**	Thank students for coming and introduce the warm-up
(optional)	**Highlights and Do-Overs**	
	Review	
8 mins	**Warm-up: (Title)**	
6 mins	**Pre Assessment**	

	Introduction	A. Who are we?
		
		Tell your story:
		
		    ❑ Who are you?
		
		    ❑ Where are you from?
		
		    ❑ Why do you do this work?
		
		B. What is TMP?
		
		    1. TMP is a Mentoring and Leadership Development Program.
		
		    2. TMP was established to provide guidance and support to young men.
		
		    3. Our Motto: "Manhood is about being present, and not being perfect."

"Manhood is about being present, not perfect." –Phil Black

268

		4. Five Virtues (or principles): Love, Respect, Courage, Provision, and Protection. *Ask if students have any questions.
	Break	
	Session Introduction	1. Overview: Our first session is simply about gaining an understanding of the program and establishing expectations. 2. Objectives: Have a volunteer read the objectives. Provide any clarity you feel is needed. 3. Agenda: After the objectives have been covered, reveal, and recite the agenda.
25 mins	**Lesson**	
25 mins	**Close**	Post-Assessment: Have students complete the post assessment. (6 mins) Clean-up (4 mins) Reflection (10 mins) Announcements (2 mins) Parting Pledge (2 mins)

"Manhood is about being present, not perfect." –Phil Black

Resources

"Manhood is about being present, not perfect." –Phil Black

TMP Group Norms

1. SAFE SPACE: The TMP group session is a sacred space that is inclusive and free of judgement.

2. MAN LAW: Never share another man's business. When we come together, sensitive and personal information is often shared. To maintain our safe space, we should never share another individual's business.

3. RESPECT: We respect everyone's personal rights, experiences, and opinions.

4. N.O.S.T.U.E.S.O.:   No One Speaks Twice Until Everyone Speaks Once

5. SELF-CORRECT: Always work to correct your own behavior before anyone else does.

6. S.L.A.N.T: Sit-up, Listen, Ask Questions, Nod your head yes or no (showing through body language that you are attentive) and Track the speaker.

7. BE PRESENT: Actively Participate.

8. PHONES UP/SILENT: Phones may only be used emergencies. Should an emergency Occur, you should excuse yourself from the room. *This should not happen often for any one individual.*

9. HANDS UP/VOICES UP: When working to get everyone re-focused on the task, the Coach may use one of these strategies.

10. LEAVE IT BETTER THAN YOU FOUND IT: Make sure the designated meeting space is clean at the end of each session.

BONUS: HAVE FUN

"Manhood is about being present, not perfect." –Phil Black

Parting Pledge

Leader: "As we go…"

Group: "Keep us safe!"

Leader: "While we're apart…"

Group: "Keep us united!"

Leader: "So when we return…"

Group: "We will be even better!"

Leader: "For we are…"

Group: "SMART!"

Leader: "We are…"

Group: "STRONG!"

Leader: "We are…"

Group: "MEN!!!!"

Leader: "Manhood on three… 1, 2, 3…"

Group: "MANHOOD!!!"

"Manhood is about being present, not perfect." –Phil Black

LESSON PLAN TEMPLATE
SESSION X: Lesson Plan Template

UX.   SXX: Session Objectives

By the end of this session the learner will be able to:
1.

AGENDA

1. Sign-in

2. Snack & Chat

3. Welcome

4. Pre Assessment (optional)

5. Warm-up

6. Session Introduction
   - ❏ Overview
   - ❏ Objectives
   - ❏ Agenda

7. Lesson
   - ❏ Activity
   - ❏ Recap
   - ❏ Norms
   - ❏ Expectations

8. Close
   - ❏ Clean-up
   - ❏ Reflection
   - ❏ Announcements
   - ❏ Parting Pledge

"Manhood is about being present, not perfect." –Phil Black

273

ACTIVITIES

ROOM SET-UP	MATERIALS NEEDED
Full or Half Circle Seating	1. Flipchart Paper 2. Dry Erase Board 3. Printing Paper 4. Markers 5. Pens

SESSION PREP

1. Ensure sign-in sheet is available.

2. Print:
   - ❏ Pre and post assessments
   - ❏ Copies of opening and closing pledge

3. Set-up transition music.

4. Make sure snacks are ready for distribution.

5. *Write* and post: Objectives, Agenda, Norms & Expectations, and Review Questions on separate sheets of flipchart paper. *If Dry Erase Board is available, use it to write session objectives. Reserve flipchart for the other information.*

"Manhood is about being present, not perfect." –Phil Black

SESSION DETAILS		
1.5 - 2 hr		
	Pre-Session	Set up all materials and music.
3 mins	**Sign-in**	Have students sign in as they enter the designated space.
15 mins	**Snack & Chat**	
3 mins	**Welcome**	Thank students for coming and introduce the warm-up
(optional)	**Highlights and Do-Overs**	
	Review	
8 mins	**Warm-up: (Title)**	
6 mins	**Pre Assessment**	
	Introduction	
	Break	
	Session Introduction	
25 mins	**Lesson**	
25 mins	**Close**	Post-Assessment: Have students complete the post assessment. (6 mins) Clean-up (4 mins) Reflection (10 mins) Announcements (2 mins) Parting Pledge (2 mins)

"Manhood is about being present, not perfect." –Phil Black

BONUS SESSION: Locker Room

Description

This session titled "Locker Room" was specifically designed for programming flexibility and to also meet the needs of a broad audience of participants. As the name suggests, Locker Room is a designated time completely devoted to discussing personal challenges, exploring random ideas, or current events. Locker Room is basically a time to take a mental break from the structured and academic format of the program. This time is intended to provide a safe space for students to receive advice from you (as their facilitator/coach) and from their peers- to aide in team building. Locker Room sessions usually happen once every 8 to 10 sessions. As the facilitator, it will be your job to determine when a session time is most appropriate. Below is a list of best practices used for the locker room session.

AGENDA

While we encourage you to maintain the core elements of the session format (e.g. Snack & Chat, Lesson/Activity and Close), the majority of the agenda is up to you. Here are two examples:

Agenda 1
Snack & Chat
Real Talk (students are allowed to submit topics of discussion not regularly addressed)
Team Building (for the second half of the session)
Reflection/Close

Agenda 2
Snack & Chat
Team Building (for the entire session)
Close

Best Practices

- ❑ Round Table Talks
- ❑ Current events
- ❑ Snap Debates
- ❑ Board Games
- ❑ Video Games
- ❑ Open Gym
- ❑ Outdoor Activities

ROOM SET-UP	ADDITIONAL NOTE
Reflective of the activities chosen.	As Locker Room is a special session, we typically bring special snacks or a full meal.

"Manhood is about being present, not perfect." –Phil Black

GUEST SPEAKER
GUEST SPEAKER TEMPLATE

AGENDA

1. Sign-in

2. Snack & Chat

3. Welcome/Overview

4. Introduction of Speaker (reminder of Norms)

5. Guest Speaker

6. Q&A

7. Final Thoughts

8. Close
   - ❑ Clean-up
   - ❑ Reflection
   - ❑ Announcements
   - ❑ Parting Pledge

ACTIVITIES

ROOM SET-UP	MATERIALS NEEDED
Full or Half Circle Seating	1. If requested by speaker

SESSION PREP

1. Ensure sign-in sheet is ready.
2. Make sure snacks are ready to distribute.
3. Prepare, if any, materials from speaker that were requested

"Manhood is about being present, not perfect." –Phil Black

SESSION DETAILS		
1.5 - 2 hrs		
	Pre-Session	Set up all materials and music.
3 mins	**Sign-in**	Have students sign in as they enter the designated space.
15 mins	**Snack & Chat**	
3 mins	**Welcome/ Overview**	
1 - 3 mins	**Introduction of Speaker**	*Remind students of Norms
	Guest Speaker	
	Q&A	
	Final Thoughts	
8 mins	**Close**	Clean-up (4 mins) Announcements (2 mins) Parting Pledge (2 mins)

"Manhood is about being present, not perfect." –Phil Black

Speaker Question Guide

Questions to consider/answer during the guest speaker's speech

While these specific questions may be used to format your discussion, feel free to add your own. These questions are simply a guide.

1. Who are you? (Name, place of birth, etc.)

2. What do you do professionally, and what does it entail?

3. How did you get to where you are?

4. What was life like for you growing up, or at the age of the audience?

5. What type of student were you?

6. Did you have a life changing moment? If so, what was it?

7. Who influenced you?

8. How did you overcome adversity in your life? (Give at least one example.)

9. What lessons have you learned? (Up to 3 but no more than 5, if making specific bullet points)

10. What does: "You don't have to be perfect, but you do have to be present" mean to you? Or how does that motto connect with your personal experience?

"Manhood is about being present, not perfect." –Phil Black

Guest Speaker Facilitation Tips

1. **Be yourself**
   When connected to the speaker, students receive the most from conversations and engage easily. Often times, while attempting to increase communication and social skills of young adults, we (as speakers, mentors…) unknowingly create barriers- by presenting an overly polished image of ourselves. It is good to know who you have become, but it is better to learn from the *process* of how you became.

2. **Support TMP norms.**
   Try to support/use the norms of the program when needed or most applicable.

3. **Know your audience**
   When engaging, keep in mind the age and mindset of the target audience. Some students may lack proper communication etiquette. With that said, you may hear language or comments that (in other environments) would be deemed inappropriate or offensive. In order to teach them better, we must first make students comfortable enough to show their true selves, then offer alternative behaviors.

4. **Assume the best**
   Unless a student makes an overt negative or offensive comment (especially with malicious intent), always assume the best. Meaning, they may not know any better- which is why we are here to help.

5. **Leave the gavel**
   This is a no judgment zone. We have found that most students tend to easily adapt to their environment. Meaning, they are most likely to self-correct certain behaviors (e.g. language and other social norms) over time and with practice. One thing to stay away from (in a round table environment especially) is attempting to openly correct a student in front of their peers, or doing anything that makes the student feel isolated or attacked. This often creates a hostile environment. In the rare case that a student's behavior is continuously unacceptable, we will then remove him from the space.

6. **Use dialog or open ended questions, rather than absolute statements**
   Unless you are sharing a brief narrative of your personal experience, try to refrain from making absolute statements. Remember, the object is to "guide" the student's thinking- not dictate their thoughts.

"Manhood is about being present, not perfect." –Phil Black

7. **Be prepared, yet flexible.**

While we have a set agenda and objectives for the program, we've found that the best Round Table Discussions evolve organically. These discussions are typically formed as the result of of a statement, or an unforeseen question raised by one of the students. Please be prepared for the talk, but remain flexible at the same time.

8. **Remain focused on the current objective.**

We will aim to move seamlessly throughout the conversation, making sure that there will be specific times for certain comments. For example, when sharing our experiences we encourage speakers to save "the final lessons" or desired take-aways until the end of the workshop.

9. **Keep the appropriate balance.**

As mentioned previously, aside from sharing our personal experiences, the goal is to provide a space for students to be heard. After we have shared our stories, the talk ratio should shift from being 100/0% (speaker/student) to 40-60% in favor of the students.

10. **Enjoy it.**

Lastly, at the end of the day, enjoy yourself. This is a great opportunity to reach back and connect with a group of individuals looking for you guidance. Show them who you are, and have fun doing it.

"Manhood is about being present, not perfect." –Phil Black

Guest Speaker Student Notes

Speaker Name:
Occupation/Job:
From (City, State, School, etc.)**:**

Notes:

1. What I liked most about the speaker's presentation was:

2. I have learned:

3. I would like to know:

"Manhood is about being present, not perfect." –Phil Black

ONE-ON-ONES
Initial One-on-One Template

Session Objectives

By the end of this session the facilitator will be able to:

1. Share brief information about yourself as the facilitator/coach of the program and why you have chosen to do this work.

2. Gain basic information from the students about themselves and gauge their level of understanding about coaching and the program in general.

3. Determine how having a coach and participating in the program may benefit the student from their own perspective.

4. Highlight desired outcomes and expectations, while receiving the expectations of the student.

AGENDA

1. Intro

2. Purpose of Meeting

3. Personal Story

4. The Student

5. Expectations

6. Questions

7. Next Steps

8. Conclusion

"Manhood is about being present, not perfect." –Phil Black

SESSION DETAILS		
20 – 35 mins		
2 – 3 mins	**Intro**	Build basic rapport with the student by asking about their day, week, etc. Welcome and congratulate them on being selected to the program.
1 – 2 mins	**Purpose**	Explain the purpose of the meeting by sharing: 1. The objectives. (in common language) 2. An overview of what will be covered. 3. How having one on one time will help in the overall relationship and process of working together. 1-2 minutes
2 – 5 mins	**Personal Story**	Talk about: 1. Who you are. 2. Where you are from. 3. Your professional background. 4. What drew you to this work? 5. Why you are interested in working with them specifically
5 – 8 mins	**The Student**	*Ask*: 1. What do you know about the program and why do you feel that you were selected? In the event a student responds: "I don't know"- ask, If you had to guess, what would be the reasons? *The goal is to get them to express any particular challenges that they may be facing (if they have been referred to the program for a specific reason). 2. What is a coach? *Student should attempt to make the connection between an athletic coach and a life coach to explain the relationship. The main point being, a life coach prepares you in the same way an athletic coach does- the difference being, we prepare you for the game of everyday life and experiences (at home, school and society in

"Manhood is about being present, not perfect." –Phil Black

284

		general).
		3. In what ways do you feel a life coach or working with the program can benefit you? Here, explain the general expectations you have for the student with regards to their experience working within the program and their outcomes. While discussing general norms such as being an active participant, showing respect and so forth are encouraged, try to stay away from going too far in depth. Also ask, what are the expectations of the student?
1 – 3 mins	**Questions**	Allow time for general questions
8 mins	**Next Steps**	Share the logistics of the program and what the next steps are within the process.
6 mins	**Conclusion**	Thank the student and express your joy for having them participate.

Ongoing One-on-One Template

Session Objectives
By the end of this session the facilitator will be able to:

1. Assess students overall feelings about the program and his participation.

2. Evaluate student's progress towards goals.

3. Set goals for next meeting.

AGENDA

1. Intro

2. Praise

3. Observations

4. Evaluation

5. Goal Setting

6. Questions

"Manhood is about being present, not perfect." –Phil Black

SESSION DETAILS		
15 – 35 mins		
2 – 3 mins	**Intro**	Build basic rapport with the student by asking about their day, week, etc.
1 – 2 mins	**Purpose**	Explain the purpose of the meeting by sharing: 1. The objectives (in common language) 2. An overview of what will be covered and 3. How having one on one time will help ensure the student will meet his goals.
3 – 6 mins	**Praise**	Identify one or more areas to praise the student in their progress or participation within the program. Give specific examples when the student may have shown leadership, helped someone, or simply followed directions regularly. Note: This praise must be genuine and authentic. If the student has not done anything praiseworthy, do not feel obligated.
2 – 3 mins	**Observations**	Discuss any pertinent observations (positive or potentially challenging). Ask relevant questions. Example: Mark, I've noticed that you are becoming more focused within the sessions and participating regularly. What has changed to make you want to become more involved?
4 – 6 mins	**Evaluation**	Review the most recent progress report, report card, behavior report and or teacher feedback with the student. Ask follow up questions to assess their level of satisfaction.
2 – 5 mins	**Goal Setting**	Have the student to set 1-3 SMART goals related to their personal life, academics, and behavior.
2 – 5 mins	**Questions**	Allow time for student questions and comments.
	Next Steps	Give final remarks and discuss upcoming lessons/trips.
	Conclusion	Thank the student and express your joy for having them participate.

"Manhood is about being present, not perfect." –Phil Black

I am

I am…

"I am" statements are used to describe how you personally view yourself. Now that you've completed the program, how would you describe yourself using an "I am" statement? Write 10 "I am…" statements based on those personal views.

1. I am

2. I am

3. I am

4. I am

5. I am

6. I am

7. I am

8. I am

9. I am

10. I am

"Manhood is about being present, not perfect." –Phil Black

Reflection

If someone were to review all of your "I am" statements, would they think that you have a positive or negative image of yourself? Explain your answer.

I am NOT

I am not…

"I am not" statements are the direct opposite of "I am" statements, and are more of a reflection of how others view you. Write 5 "I am not…" statements based on what others or society may have used to describe you at some point.

1. I am not

2. I am not

3. I am not

4. I am not

5. I am not

Reflection

How do your "I am" statements compare to your "I am not" statements?

What thoughts come to mind after writing both kinds of statements?

"Manhood is about being present, not perfect." –Phil Black

Letter to Self

To assist ones self during tough times in life, and to remind ones self as to why continuously working on self is important, write a letter of encouragement to yourself.

_____

_____

_____

_____

_____

_____

_____

_____

_____

_____

_____

_____

_____

_____

_____

_____

_____

_____

_____

_____

"Manhood is about being present, not perfect." –Phil Black

_____

_____

_____

_____

_____

_____

_____

_____

_____

_____

_____

_____

_____

_____

_____

(Sign and Date)

"Manhood is about being present, not perfect." –Phil Black

My Values

Make a list of everything that is important to you.

1. _____
   What makes this important?

2. _____
   What makes this important?

3. _____
   What makes this important?

4. _____
   What makes this important?

5. _____
   What makes this important?

"Manhood is about being present, not perfect." –Phil Black

6. _____

What makes this important?

7. _____

What makes this important?

8. _____

What makes this important?

Assessing My Rep

The Linebacker Coach and team recruiter for Penn State University has decided to come and watch you play in the last game of the season. After viewing your game, both were incredibly impressed with your on field performance- so much so, that they've decided to look at your records and interview a few people that are close to you.

What will the coach and recruiter find in your file? What will the individuals interviewed have to say about you? Be extremely detailed and honest, and write exactly what might be found in your file.

File

Overall GPA: _____

Most Recent Card Marking: _____

Number of classes missed per week (on average): _____

Late to class (per week): _____

Referrals: _____

Suspensions: _____

Counselor:

Math Teacher:

"Manhood is about being present, not perfect." –Phil Black

English Teacher:

Principal:

Position Coach:

Head Coach:

Mother:

Permission Slip Example

By signing this document I give my son _____ full permission to attend The Manhood Project day-trip to *Michigan State University* on *April 23rd, 2016*. The student contribution is *$10* and will help cover *transportation, meals/snacks,* and a *souvenir tee-shirt*. I understand that there will be a Parent Briefing sent home by *April 20th* which will include the full itinerary, permitted and prohibited items, expectations, and code of conduct. I can also log on to the *TMP* site: *www.tmpmentoring.com* for details. *TMP* will only pick up and drop off students at the designated locations/schools according to the schedule below.

All students who are looking to ride the bus must be at the pick-up location on time.

School/Pick-up Location	Students will board bus by	Departing Time
Cody	7:00am	7:10am
Central	7:30am	7:40am
Madison High	8:00am	8:10am
Brenda Scott	7:30am	7:40am

We will return to each school at the times below:

School/Drop off Location	Drop off Time
Madison	7:00pm
Central	7:30pm
Cody-APL	8:00pm
Brenda Scott	7:00pm

I give permission for my child _____ to attend *Michigan State University on April 23, 2016*.

I have also included the *$10* student contribution.

Instructions for my child:

Parent/Guardian:

Name:

Phone:

Emergency Contact: _____ Phone: _____

_____
Parent/Guardian signature

_____
Date

"Manhood is about being present, not perfect." –Phil Black

Notes:

Printed in Great Britain
by Amazon